STUFF IRISH PEOPLE LOVE

The definitive guide to the unique
passions of the Paddies

Colin Murphy & Donal O'Dea

THE O'BRIEN PRESS
DUBLIN

First published 2011 by The O'Brien Press Ltd
12 Terenure Road East, Rathgar, Dublin 6, Ireland.
Tel: +353 1 4923333; Fax; +353 1 4922777
Email: books@obrien.ie; Website: www.obrien.ie

ISBN: 978-1-84717-285-3

1 2 3 4 5 6 7 8
11 12 13 14 15 16

Cover design: Donal O'Dea

Printed and bound by MPG Books Ltd
The paper used in this book is produced using pulp from managed forests

Thanks to:
Kathryn Murphy, John Williams, Gerry McCloskey, Brendan
O'Reilly, Paul (Turty-tree and a turd) Moran, Oran and Keith
Nevin, Olive Cogan, Emma Everard, Adrian Cosgrove, Pauline
Murphy, Stephen McKeon, Sara Al-Uzaizi, Rob O'Dea, Tom &
Will Foley, Mary Webb, Fiona Field and John Gildea who all
contributed to this book.
And to: Gerrit Quast, Simon Fitzpatrick (www.leinsterman.com),
George Keith, Felix 'O'(Sludgegulper) agus Gary Knight for the
use of their photos.

1 Marietta biscuit butter sandwiches with the butter squeezed through.

For those who don't know what a Marietta biscuit is … well it's sort of like a Rich Tea biscuit with lots of little holes in it. And back in the days when we were all poor, as distinct from utterly bankrupt, most people only rarely bought fancy biscuits with a filling, as they put too much of a strain on the grocery bill. So the next best thing was to butter two Marietta biscuits and stick them together. In fact, if you put on enough butter and pressed them tightly, the butter would squeeze

through the little holes like tiny worms … yummy. Ironically, buttering the Marietta probably made the biscuits more expensive than standard fancy ones. Since then we've come a long way and most homes are packed with double-choc-cream-crisp strawberry delights, or some other fancy oul' shite biscuits. But secretly, when they're alone, most Irish people will still sneak into the kitchen and butter themselves a couple of Marietta when nobody's watching. And if you're really degenerate, you might even dunk your buttered Mariettas into your cup of tea before sucking down the soggy, buttery mess. Heaven.

 ## Scraping shite off boots with a stick.

This is particular to Irish country folk, farming folk specifically. Thanks to the fact that the heavens are always opening on us and we have more sheep and cows than people, Ireland's lanes and boreens are frequently almost invisible beneath a thick layer of mud and cowshite, much of which gathers on the soles of our farming brothers and sisters who toil on the land. So the sight of farmers poking the shite off their boots with a stick outside pubs, houses and shops in country villages is pretty ubiquitous.

The secret to successful shite-scraping is to get

a 'good firem shtick' that ta-
pers to a solid point that can
get at the shite in the narrow
grooves on the soles of
wellies.

At least 90% of the shite
must be removed before it is
considered proper etiquette to
enter an establishment,

thereby leaving only a thin veneer of cowshite on
the pub or bedroom carpet.

Nicknaming our public statues.

Irish people, Dubliners in particular,
love to slag the crap out of their new public statues
by christening them with amusing or smutty
rhyming nicknames. This has become quite a com-
petitive sport, and often the same monument or

statue is blessed with four or five different sobri-
quets. The practice seems to have started with the
erection of a piece of public sculpture in Dublin's
O'Connell Street for the celebration of The Dublin
Millennium in 1988. This work, called Anna Livia,
was supposed to personify the River Liffey and
featured a woman lying in a bubbling froth of water.
This became a gathering place for drunken youths
(as opposed to now, when the entire city centre is
a gathering place for drunken youths) and within
weeks of its appearance, some wag had
nicknamed it 'The Floozie in the Jacuzzi'. If only
they had known what they were starting. Soon afterwards, Anna Livia had a second nickname: 'The
Hoor in the Sewer'. Eventually the poor oul'
'Floozie' was relocated to The Croppy Acre Memo-
rial Park outside Collins Barracks, where she was
renamed 'The Floozie without the Jacuzzi'.

Her spot in O'Connell Street was taken by The
Spire of Dublin in 2003, which in a blink was
re-christened 'The Stiletto in the Ghetto', 'The Nail
in the Pale' 'The Stiffy in the Liffey', 'The Rod to
God' and most popularly 'The Erection at the
Intersection.' By Jaysus, there was no stopping us

now … no statue or monument was safe from the critical eye of the Dublin jokesmiths.

A statue representing the ordinary people and featuring two old dears with shopping bags near The Ha'penny Bridge was renamed 'The Hags with the Bags'. One of James Joyce in North Earl Street has been dubbed 'The Prick with the Stick' and a colourful one of Oscar Wilde reclining on a rock in Merrion Square has been called 'The Queer with

the Leer', 'The Fag on the Crag' or 'The Quare in the Square.'

The poet Patrick Kavanagh's statue by the canal is known as 'The Crank on the Bank' and a disastrous attempt to place a giant clock in the Liffey that was to count-down to the millennium (the water got into the works) was nicknamed

'The Time in the Slime'.

But in the nicknaming stakes, champion of

champions has to be the statue of the fishmonger famed in song, Molly Malone. The Grafton Street bronze monument affords us a fine view of Molly's ginormous cleavage. According to the song, poor Molly died of a fever, but she might have died of embarrassment had she known she would one day be known variously as 'The Tart with the Cart', 'The Dolly with the Trolley', 'The Dish with the Fish', 'The Flirt in the Skirt' or 'The Trollop with the Scallops'!

 A big lump of vanilla ice cream dropped into a glass of fizzy orange or cola.

If you're not Irish, we can hear you gasp in astonishment/revulsion at the very notion. But while the French were spending hours creating things like *Emincé de Volaille sauce Roquefort avec pommes de terre sautées,* we were cutting thick slices off a block of cheap vanilla ice-cream and plonking them into a big pint glass of fizzy orange or cola and then either eating the resultant frothing gloop with a spoon, or the less refined of us were trying to glug the entire thing down straight from the glass. The taste … ah, the taste … was all at once icy, fizzy, orangey/cola-ish and messy … it had that certain *je ne sais quoi,* or as we say in Ireland, *an-mhaith ar fad!*

 Inserting swearwords into the middle of other words.

Irish people swear a lot. If you're Irish you're probably responding to that statement by saying something like 'So bleedin' wha?' On the other hand, visitors to these shores are often taken aback at the casual way we use swear words in the most innocuous situations. Here's a simple example:

'Would you like a coffee, Fiona?'

'Thanks, Mick. Are there any fuckin' digestives?'

But that's mild by Irish standards. If you're a foreigner, don't be alarmed if you overhear sentences like the one below, where a typical Irishman arranges a social engagement:

'Howya Deco, ye bollox ye. C'mere, I fancy getting' bleedin' rat-arsed down de fuckin' local 'cause that dickhead Willie was givin' me a pain in the hole all day at work and I was up te me tits in shite.'

Anyone Irish overhearing this conversation would not even blink twice at the profanity. However, where we Irish have pioneered the art of swearing is in our unique ability to insert swear words not just into ordinary sentences, but also inside the words themselves. To illustrate, let us repeat this paragraph, this time using said pioneering technique:

Anyone Irish overbleedinhearing this conversation would not even blink twice at the proshitinfanity. However, where we Irish have pionbleedineered the art of swearing is in our unique afuckinbility to insert swearbleedinwords not just into ordinary sentences, but also inside the words themfuckinselves.

With such linguistic creativity, is it any wonder we gave the world James Joyce, George Bernard Shaw, William Butler Yeats etc?

6 Jackeens saying 'that's a grand healthy smell' when they get a whiff of cowshite.

Without fail, poor Dublin eejits out for a day's drive in the countryside will always remark on the 'grand healthy smell' or the 'fine country aroma', after which they will breathe in sharply to make sure they capture a complete lungful of the 'precious air'.

Actually, the smell coming from the other side of the ditch is usually either of silage, which is rotting, putrid hay, or just plain old cowshite, which is probably buzzing with bluebottles and likely a source of several thousand different diseases. Only Irish people could warm so much to something rancid, fetid, nauseating, stomach churning and puke inducing, which probably explains why we elected Fianna Fáil into power three times in a row.

7 Contracting names by using 'o', 'ser', 'y' or 'ie'.

We love doing this. If your Mammy adored the name Anthony and had her little bundle of joy christened thus – tough shite – because before he's out of nappies Anthony will have been re-christened 'Anto'. So too will Anto's brother, Michael, who is now 'Micko', not to mention their cousin Declan, who has become 'Deco'. Aidan is 'Aido', Derek is 'Derro' and Seamus has become 'Shaymo'. The reasons for doing this are threefold:

1) Having your name abbreviated in this fashion is usually a sign of affection or friendship.
2) Irish people are informal in the extreme.
3) Irish people are too lazy to expend energy on excess and varied syllables.

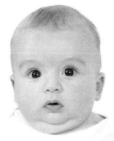

Deco

If your name doesn't suit the 'o' construction, don't worry, we'll find some sort of abbreviation suitable for you no matter who you are. Some more examples follow:

Brendan	- Breno/Brenner
Bridget	- Biddy/Breege
Cathleen	- Catty/Cateser
Desmond	- Dessie
Donal	- Donie
Denis	- Dinny
Sean	- Seany
Thomas	- Tomser/Toss

Similarly, even foreigners can be adapted to the Irish system with comparative ease. So Barack Obama would become 'Rackser', Ghandi would become 'Gando', Nelson Mandela would be lovingly greeted with the appellation 'Neller' or 'The Neller', Tony Blair as 'Tonser' and Margaret Thatcher would be known as 'That oul' Geebag.' And we don't stop at people's names. Dublin Corporation is commonly known as 'The Corpo' and Mountjoy Jail ironically as 'The Joy'.

Another naming oddity is the addition of the

word 'Óg', meaning 'young', but more like the American use of 'Junior'. So you have Sean Óg, Micheál Óg etc, to distinguish little lads from their daddies of the same name. Unfortunately, the 'Óg' will stick, even to the day when 'young' Sean kicks the bucket at the age of 102!

Reading death notices in the newspaper or listening to death notices on the radio.

(See also 'Your Ma or Da greeting you with the phrase "D'ye know who's dead?" and 'Going to funerals'.)

As children, most Irish people found it a bit disturbing to witness their parents, particularly their mothers, eagerly reading down through the columns of death notices in the daily paper. If you inquired about the reason behind this morbid practice, the usual response was 'To see who's dead'. This may sound like an obvious answer, but it came out in the same tone as 'To see who's getting hitched' or 'To see who's having an

extramarital fling' or 'To see who's pregnant'. It was
as though some poor gobshite kicking the bucket
gave one's parents a good excuse for a bit of juicy
gossip. The cause of death was also eagerly
reported. Fatal diseases of the liver always
prompted a sad shaking of the head – 'Ah, Joe
was always too fond of the drink.' Premature heart
attacks, particularly in women, suggested a life of
scandal – 'Sure it's a wonder that one lasted as
long as she did with the way she carried on.'

Reading the death columns is largely a ... eh ...
dying phenomenon in urban Ireland, but this morbid
interest was granted fresh life in most rural areas
with the advent of widespread local radio in the
nineties. The first time you hear this can be quite
startling. You're driving happily through the wilds
and you start fiddling with the radio dial looking for
a blast of Oasis or Green Day, when suddenly you
hear this deathly sombre voice saying:

*'Patrick Dunne of Ballynacarra passed away on
Tuesday. Sadly missed by his loving wife and four-
teen children. Wake in the Dunne household on
Tuesday night. Beer, whiskey and vol-au-vents sup-
plied. Funeral on Wednesday to St. Catherine's*

Cemetery.' Ok, confession time – the bit about the beer is made up. The reader will continue in this vein for so long that you'll begin to wonder if the population of the area has been wiped out by some virulent plague. Out of morbid fascination, most people will listen to just a few of these before resuming the search for Kings of Leon, but you can be sure the locals in the cottages all about are sitting glued to their radios, waiting to hear which poor eejit has popped his clogs, as though they're listening to a cliffhanger in some ghastly soap opera.

Deaths

Brady, Mary. Belturbet, Cavan.Peacefuly at home. Funeral Tuesday.PS. VW Polo for sale 60,000 on the clock. NCT, Taxed to December, Silver. All offers considered

So what is this Irish fascination with hearing about other people croaking it? Perhaps it's the Mark Twain approach. He used to read the obituary column every morning and if he wasn't in it he carried on as usual. So before you decide to head out for that pint, perhaps you should consider switching on the radio…

Unmarried couples sleeping in separate bedrooms when visiting their parents even though they've been living together for years.

Even in these sexually liberated days, many young Irish fellas and cailíns will baulk at offending their parents' sensibilities and settle for a few days of near celibacy while visiting their respective parents, even though they've been sharing an apartment and bonking away nightly for five years.

Perhaps it's the sight of the holy pictures still adorning their childhood homes that puts the fear of God into them again and fills them with sudden inexplicable guilt and a need to go to confession and tell of their exploits with the sex toys they bought on the internet. Or perhaps it's simply the way your Irish Mammy might fix you with her steely glare beneath arching eyebrows as she informs you, without debate: *'I've put Fiona in the back room, Michael. Sure you can just bed down on the sofa, can't ye?'*

I mean, in the name of Jaysus, are you really going to argue with her?

If you get desperate at some point you can always sneak into one another's room in the middle of the night for a bit of covert hanky-panky. But for some reason things don't seem to have the same zip or pzazz about them. And you know why, don't you? You can bet your bottom dollar that your mammy is lying awake through the night, with ears peeled for any inappropriate grunting and groaning, and you can just feel her x-ray eyes boring through the walls at the sight of your bare arse…

10 Culchies* heading to Dublin to do their Christmas Shopping on 8th December.

December 8th is The Feast of the Immaculate Conception, in case you'd forgotten. And it was traditionally a day of great celebration among Catholic schoolchildren – as the little feckers got the day off school. Unfortunately you had to first pay the small price of going to Mass, but then you usually had your first foretaste of the delights of Christmas as you went to visit Santa in the local shopping centre and got a toy off him that fell apart by teatime.

It also became the day, since time immemorial, when all the culchie mammies would take advantage of the kids being off school to drag them all up to Dublin – 'the big shmoke' – to do their Christmas shopping. Bemused Jackeens'* ears would be assaulted by strange accents from the nation's most remote outposts:

'A-rrr-ou goin' te Clerys?'
'Ah, will ye shtop at me, Tim Pat!'
'Gowanouttadat Bridget or ah'll skelp yer arse!'

'Horse dat inte ye, ye langer!'

Of course, the fine people of rural Ireland were always made very welcome in the capital, especially as they spent so much money, (all Jackeens suspect that every culchie in Ireland is secretly rich and constantly putting on the poor mouth).

Despite the fact that Ireland now has a major shopping centre for approximately every five people in the state, the annual influx continues unabated. Sure it's a grand day out, they'll say, while in the same breath informing you that Dublin is the greatest kip on the planet.

*For overseas readers, a 'culchie' is a person of rural extraction and a 'Jackeen' is a person from Dublin.

11 Seeing England being beaten by anybody at anything.

Are we really that pathetic that, due to matters long consigned to the history books, we take such pleasure in seeing our closest neighbours and friends over in England get beaten at anything from The Eurovision Song Contest to the European Under-11 Tiddlywinks Championship?

Yes, you bet, absolutely, 100%, we are that pathetic. And we love it! And while it's all the better if we're the ones doing the beating, it's not critical. England v Germany in football? We Irish can sing 'Deutschland über alles' like we're Bavarian. England v Azerbaijan in synchronised swimming? We'll roar ourselves hoarse like we were all born in Xacmaz! England versus the All Blacks in rugby?

Just watch us do the Irish version of the haka!

But surely as a people we're all mature enough at this stage to let historical bygones be bygones? Well, we pretend we are when we greet English visitors to our shores with a big smile and a hand-shake. But then, as soon as their backs are turned, out come the chants of '800 years of oppression!'

When it comes to sport in Ireland, it's not the winning that matters, it's the taking England apart.

 Eejits with no teeth appearing on game shows like 'Winning Streak'.

In most other countries, ordinary Joe Soaps who appear on television (mostly on game shows) are usually vetted in some fashion, or certainly some effort is made to ensure a certain minimal presentability before the individual is paraded before the watching millions. Not so in Ireland, where we much prefer our game show contestants warts and all. Literally. In fact, you'd be forgiven for thinking that TV producers actually discriminate in favour of people with warts.

And if you want to make a lasting impression on Irish TV, it certainly help if you've got just one rotten tooth clinging precariously to your upper gum. Having a wild shock of greasy hair will also add to your appeal, as will a jumper with holes  the size of your hand or a jacket collar with so much dandruff that it looks like you've just been confettied at a wedding.

To be a big small-screen success it is also essential that you plant twenty of your pals in the audience, each of whom has an arse the width of a small car and bosoms the size of basketballs. And that's just the men. Your supporters will yell things like 'YeeehoowwyeeboyyyeMick!' every time you do something right and wave placards made from cornflake boxes that urge you towards success with inspiring slogans like 'Come on Mick,' written in the green emulsion that was left over after they painted their jacks.

And if Mick wins the five grand or the Ford Fiesta? Well, holy God…

13 Having twelve+ children.

There's an old joke that tells of how the Pope hears of an Irish woman who's had twelve children, and sends a special envoy to her home to congratulate her on adhering so rigidly to the Catholic Church's teaching on contraception. But when the envoy arrives, the woman tells him there's been some mistake, as she's actually a Protestant. To which the Pope's envoy recoils in horror and exclaims, 'What? You filthy sex maniac!'

Sadly, therein lies so much truth.

Nowadays Ireland may conform largely to international norms, i.e. we have 2.4763 children per couple, but in the dark old days when the

Church ruled the roost, our average was nearer 12.3467 per couple. It was actually quite common for mothers to rear an entire hurling team of 'childer', often in a two-bedroom house with no indoor plumbing. The writer Christy Brown's mother famously gave birth to 22 nippers, 13 of whom survived. Just imagine the chaos in the mornings trying to get into the jacks!

Then there's the financial impact of trying to feed and clothe the little beggars. 'You'll have te put more water in the soup' was common advice as families swelled.

Through necessity, a hand-me-down culture also flourished. Pity the poor little youngest guy after he's been handed down a pair of jocks that have had his seven older brothers' arses through

them before he gets to don them. Or the unfortunate girl who has a 36-inch bust and has to
squeeze into the size 32A bra she inherited from
her older sister.

But why, you may ask, would Irish people (the
mammies in particular) inflict such misery on
themselves? The Church's advice on controlling
family size was essentially to keep one's baser
urges under control and offer it up as a sacrifice to
God. Clearly we've never been very good at the
baser urge control thing, particularly the men. And
of course because the Church cloaked sex in so
much secrecy and referred to it with such terms as
'sinful carnal pleasures', everybody was just bust-
ing a gut to indulge themselves all the more. So
essentially, as soon as a couple were married,

they'd indulge themselves on every conceivable occasion, literally.

Having a hurling team of kids may have given many of us a penurious childhood, but there is a theory that the cram-packed household was one of the reasons the Irish as a race developed the gift of the gab. Think about it. Just to get someone to pass the salt above the noise of the multitude of conversations around the dinner table would have required a feat of linguistic genius.

The thing is, as the family grew bigger and bigger, the poor ould' Ma and Da would become so stressed that they'd often retire to bed just for a bit of peace. And the next thing you know...

Explaining hurling to foreigners.

Hurling is undoubtedly a sport that demands incredible skill, total fitness and in-comparable dedication. Men soar skyward and clasp a sliotar from thin air, they feint, they dodge, they hurtle across the field with the sliotar seeming glued to the end of the hurleys, they shrug off the wild swings of desperate opponents, they pivot and turn and send the sliotar sailing a mile into the sky and down between the centre of the posts … ah … a thing of beauty and grace to behold.

It's natural that we Irish, our men in particular, would take pride in explaining the intricacies of such a wonderful sport to Americans, Britons, Germans or whoever, but not because of the admiration we feel at the great skills described above. What we're actually really saying when we

boast about hurling is that you, Johnny Foreigner, are a WIMP and me, Mick the Irishman, is a REAL MAN.

American Football players so padded up they look like a walking mattress – bunch of namby pamby schoolgirls. Spoiled English or German or Italian soccer players rolling around bawling when they get a tap on the ankle – Jaysus, what a pack of ladies' pink blouses. And you Kiwi or Aussie rugby players think you're tough? Let's see how long you'd last after you've had ten lumps knocked out of you with a stick of ash wrapped in metal bands.

So, to all the hurlers who put in the training, make the sacrifices and dazzle us with their skill, keep up the good work, because you are each a living monument to Irish testosterone.

 Boiled eggs in a cup mashed with a lump of butter.

Another great Irish delicacy that was handed down by our parents. In the old days we couldn't afford any fancy high-falutin' foods like cajun chicken wraps or ciabatta with red pesto – in fact we'd never even heard of them. So we invented our own peculiar little culinary indulgences. You simply boiled a couple of eggs until they were rock solid, then chopped them up in a cup while they were still warm, added some salt and tossed in a generous lump of real butter, then mixed it around until it had melted. For best results, this master-piece of Irish cuisine was then eaten with a spoon directly from the cup.

Claiming you're related to someone who fought in the GPO in the Rising.

Whenever talk in Ireland turns to the Easter Rising (which it increasingly will as the centenary draws near), it's a certain bet that one of the party will announce that his grandad or great-grand-uncle or next-door neighbour's great-grand-auntie's cat was one of the insurgents who battled for Ireland's freedom in 1916. The belief is that such a connection to the Rising's tragic heroes underscores your patriotic/Republican credentials and there's also the possibility that some of glory will rub off on you. But that's not the only reason for this phenomenon, as, secretly, a little bit of

GPO 1916

every true-blooded Irishman and woman wishes they could have actually been there taking pot shots at enemy soldiers down below in Sackville Street, or defending Boland's Mill or holding out, Alamo-style, against impossible odds in the house overlooking Mount Street Bridge as the tyrant army massed below.

The thing is, though, if all the claims of being

related to or knowing one of the volunteers in the Rising are true, then there would have been approximately 250,000 insurgents crammed into the GPO that day. If only…

Shouting 'Yeeeeeooow' in the middle of a traditional Irish tune.

Put a handful of Irish musicians together, particularly in a pub, and as sure as eggs is eggs,

as the fiddles and whistles and bodhrans begin to whip up a frenzy of rhythm, one of the musicians or someone in the audience will be com- pelled by a rising fire in his or her breast to proclaim loudly 'Yeeeeeoooow!'

Photo: George Keith

Some believe this to be the musical equivalent of an orgasm, others that it is an expression of joy that only Irish music has the ability to evoke. It is even possible, some think, that it is an expression of a deeply buried primordial scream which is given release by the thundering pace and rhythm of the music, such as a caveman might yell having just downed a wild pig with a stone axe.

Whatever the reason, there are endless variations on the word itself, the most popular being 'Yeehaaayeboyye', 'Yeeeeeeeeeeeehooo' or 'Yeeeupdereyefineting'.

 ## Changing into swimming togs under a towel on the beach.

A tradition that still survives to this day, it came about primarily because when people first started to take to the beaches en masse in the last century, unlike most other countries in the western world, Ireland was too poor to afford changing huts. So, on those rare sunny summer days, it would not be uncommon to see hundreds of people, men and women, boys and girls, struggling desperately to divest themselves of their underpants, knickers and bras and replace them with a pair of swimming togs or a bathing suit, usually accompanied by a non-stop string of grunts and profanities as the sand uncomfortably worked its way into all sorts of places not normally exposed to nature.

It was tough enough for men to do this, but for the ladies it was an absolute nightmare, possessed as they are of a more expansive spread of bits to conceal. It was necessary for the poor ladies to hold their towel awkwardly both at the top and the bottom and at the same time manoeuvre their feet through a one-piece bathing suit, find the holes for their legs and arms and then yank the garment up using a combination of fingers and teeth.

In the old days, a common pastime of young lads deprived of all forms of titillation by Ireland's censorious elders was to wander the beach in search of girls in the process of changing, in the hope that the towel might slip a few inches and reward them with a brief glimpse of forbidden female flesh, which, naturally, made the girls' job all the more difficult.

But if changing in this fashion was bad when you arrived at the beach, putting your clothes back on after a day's splashing in the surf was infinitely worse, as this time the sand clung to your wet bits and inevitably ended up inside your underwear, and, by God, did your unmentionable parts get a rough ride home at the end of the day.

Bacon and Cabbage.

Another uniquely Irish dish, although there is an American equivalent in Corned Beef and Cabbage, but once again our history of poverty dictated that if we had meat at all, it would be the cheapest – pig's meat – corned beef being the preserve of the wealthy.

Traditionally one uses a back bacon cut which is boiled to hell, and if one wishes to truly enjoy Irish bacon and cabbage as it was originally served, the chopped cabbage should be tossed in with the bacon and allowed to cook until it has essentially turned into a mush of salty slop, the smell of which would keep strangers from your door for a week.

20 Begrudgery.

Ireland has three national sports: Gaelic football, hurling and begrudgery. Many Irish people are surprised to learn that 'begrudgery' is a word little known outside these shores and doesn't appear in most standard English reference dictionaries.

It is uniquely Irish.

Begrudgery, for any overseas reader, involves deeply resenting any success or wealth achieved by anyone, especially if they're a fellow Irish person. It is not confined to resentment of the rich and powerful, but is most commonly observed among the closest of friends and associates.

An example might be if your best friend has been unemployed for a year, meriting your sympathy, until said friend gets a job that pays slightly more than your own. Rather than expressing happiness that his luck has turned a corner, according to tradition Irish people in this situation will force a 'congratulations' through clenched teeth and mutter 'jammy bastard' to themselves.

When it comes to the truly successful, whether in the fields of business, politics, music, sport, movies, or whatever, almost all Irish men and women could give a master class in begrudgery. Spotting, say, a famous Irish rock star eating in a posh restaurant will usually prompt a look of disgust and a phrase like 'It's far from vintage wine that fecker was rared'. Irrespective of whether they earned their wealth and fortune through hard work and talent, instead of admiring the successes of others, the Irish instinctively wish to drag the offender back to their own level and 'put him/her in their proper place'.

The roots of this curious Irish trait are probably to be found in the fact that Ireland is, in comparison with other countries, pretty classless. So anyone deciding to better himself/herself is judged to be striving to climb above the shoulders of the entire nation and should therefore be brought low quickly.

Begrudgery also thrives because it provides hours of entertainment in the pub as we each take our turns slagging off some Joe Soap who's 'gotten above himself'.

The renowned 18th century English author Samuel Johnson actually observed this curious phenomenon two centuries ago when he remarked that: *'The Irish are a very fair people. They never speak well of each other.'* But the best response to Irish begrudgery is provided appropriately by Brendan Behan with his simple and pithy *'Fuck the begrudgers.'*

A grand stretch in the evenings.

The shortest day of the year, the winter solstice, falls on December 21st or 22nd each year and, as sure as the day is long, on the day after the solstice many an Irish person will be heard to remark that 'There's a grand stretch in the evenings', despite the fact that daylight hours have only extended by roughly two minutes.

It's a phrase born of the fact that we're a nation of hopers, we Irish. We've spent literally centuries hoping for better times ahead. Hoping the English would leave us alone, hoping we'd get to heaven when we die, hoping we might get a few politicians who actually gave a damn about the country, hoping the economy might turn a corner … the list is endless.

And invariably we either end up disappointed or have to wait so long that we begin to despair.

'A grand stretch in the evenings' is our way of saying that whatever else happens, we know one thing for certain: we're about to put the misery of the damp, dank, freezing Irish winter behind us.

Of course, the Irish summers aren't usually much of an improvement, but we can always hope.

44

Boasting that we were the first country in the world to ban smoking in pubs (and then secretly cursing the politicians who did it.)

As a small nation we do love to blow our own trumpet at our minor innovations and small successes. Thus we will proudly inform foreigners that in Ireland we're so environmentally friendly we tax plastic shopping bags, or snigger at the fact that the British or the US still measure distances in miles – 'C'mon, what feckin' century are yis livin' in?', we'll ask with a smirk.

Most of all, though, we like to boast proudly that Ireland was the first nation in the world to introduce a compre- hensive smoking ban, which included pubs, restaurants and all other places of enter-

tainment. We wore a particularly smug grin as we watched all of our European neighbours follow our lead, knowing that we'd been the ones to start the dominoes toppling.

The reality is, however, that we secretly hate ourselves for doing it, or certainly the politicians who came up with the idea. This is principally because the ban has wreaked havoc with our pub culture. Bars formerly crammed wall to wall with drinkers and smokers now lie empty, the ghostly echoes of a million nights of craic fading into memory, tumbleweed blowing silently past lonely barmen and sad little groups of self-righteous anti-smoking campaigners sipping on their bitter lemons and mulling over the possibility of banning alcohol as well.

Meanwhile, the drinkers have either stayed at home and bought a six-pack where they can kill themselves in peace without some gobshite telling them that they're going to get cancer. Or else they're to be found in the smoking area, nowadays the busiest part of any pub in Ireland. There they stand, fag in one hand, pint in the other, freezing their tits off as they try desperately to do their patriotic duty and keep the spirit of the Irish pub alive. And of course their non-smoking friends have little choice but to join them and suffer the cold, leaving them bitter in their heart at Ireland's nanny state.

So, to all the other countries (particularly the cold ones) who were obliged to follow our non-smoking lead, we're really not that proud. In fact, we apologise profoundly.

 Waving hello to complete strangers on country roads.

You're cycling or walking along a remote country road in a part of Ireland you've never set foot in and the next thing a guy in a passing car raises his hand and waves at you. Was it, by some fluke, someone you knew? Then the guy in the next car does the same. And the woman passing on the tractor does the same. Pretty soon you begin to suspect you're the exact double of some local hero and you start to imagine scenarios of you arriving in town to a ticker-tape welcome and being fawned over by the local beauties or hunks, whatever your preference. Then you see someone waving at another passer-by. And another. And it begins to dawn that everybody is waving at everybody. In fact the entire area seems to have been inflicted with a per-petual arm-waving and head-nodding hysteria.

You've just discov-ered the Irish liking for friendliness and camaraderie. We really, really want to be regarded as friendly, because, well, we are actually a friendly lot when it comes down to it. This is less obvious in our cities, but even there you don't have to dig very deep to reveal the genial soul underneath the cold exterior.

Lonely Planet recently voted Ireland the friendliest nation on earth and the website Opentravel.com listed the five friendliest nations as: 5 Georgia, 4 Iran, 3 Canada, 2 Australia, 1 Ireland. Which is great, as we can really use all the tourists we can get.

Why are we so hospitable? Who knows? Maybe it's because we're generally a bit lazy as a nation and conflict is just too much like hard work. Others believe that because of all our economic woes, we take comfort in sharing our tribulations with our friends. And being friendly never cost anyone a cent.

Tayto crisps or Tayto crisp sandwiches.

A couple of years back, one of the paparazzi magazines featured a shot of an Irish movie star emerging from an Irish shop in Hollywood laden down with a box of Tayto crisps containing sixty packs. In many ways it summed up the Irish obsession with this snack food brand, in that the actor, for all his millions, still craved the simple joy of Ireland's favourite crisp. It's actually a common sight in Irish airports to see the Diaspora leaving their homeland burdened down by large boxes of

Tayto. And the general population of just four million they've left behind manage to crunch their way through roughly three-quarters of a million packs every day!

So why the obsession? Well, put simply, Irish people will tell you that Tayto are the best tasting crisps in the world and will brook no argument on the matter. American crisps, by comparison, are so bland they defy belief, and English crisps taste like deep-fried cardboard. Some have suggested that our love of Tayto is linked with the potato's place in our history (The Famine etc) but as they weren't invented until 1954, this seems unlikely. We also take pride in the fact that Joe 'Spud' Murphy, the Tayto company's founder, also invented the world's first Cheese & Onion flavoured crisp.

When certain foreign supermarkets started operating in Ireland in recent times, instead of Tayto, they stocked some unheard-of cheap crisps from God knows where. They realised soon enough that it wouldn't matter if they were actually paying people to take them off the shelves, the Irish wanted their Tayto and nothing else. The poor eejits copped on quick enough.

Tayto recently enjoyed success on the bestseller list with the brand's own book and the company have now even opened up their own theme park, called Tayto Park. And recently a Chinese entrepreneur who fell in love with the crisps while living here, launched the product in his homeland where Tayto are known as 'tudoushenshi shuping'. Quite a mouthful.

And then there's the Tayto Crisp Sandwich, another Irish delicacy. A pile of Tayto Cheese & Onion crisps sandwiched between two slices of buttered bread. Ah, that moment when it crunches thunderously just as you sink your teeth into it and savour the taste of the world's greatest crisp! Thank you, Joe Spud Murphy, one of Ireland's true heroes.

(PS The authors of this book have no connection with the Tayto company or any of its associates, but if the nice people at Tayto want to send the authors a few free packs for the nice plug, please feel free to do so.)

Saying 'Ah no I won't' three times before accepting the offer of a drink.

Right, all foreigners – get this. When you offer an Irish person a drink and he or she says, 'Ah no, I won't', DO NOT say 'ok' and turn away. The proper response is 'Are you sure?' to which the Irish person will say, 'No, I'm grand, thanks'. You should then persist with 'Go on, have the one', to which he or she will appear to fight the temptation for a few seconds before replying, 'No I better not.' Now you say, *'Gooo onnnn.'* At which point the Irish person will finally relent and then proceed to drink your house, or the bar you're in, dry.

Remember, we all love to appear as if we're a people of moderation. The problem is that we also practice moderation strictly in moderation.

Drinking tea from a flask and eating sandwiches from the boot of a car while attending away GAA matches.

Whenever Irish people's county or local GAA club are involved in an away match, it's still a common sight to see the travelling supporters huddled around their car boots slurping tea (pronounced 'tae') from a flask and chomping on sandwiches which have been kept fresh in a Johnston Mooney & O'Brien or Brennan's Bread wrapper. To complete the picture, the milk for the tea should ideally be poured from a cleaned-out Chef Sauce bottle.

In the days before we all drove on motorways, these hungry individuals were usually spotted pulled over into the hard shoulder in the middle of nowhere, four or five to a group, relishing their refreshments and saying things like, 'Ye can't bate the taste of tae and batch loaf ham sambos served from a car boot in the country air, sure ye can't,

Mick?' Nowadays the phenomenon has moved en masse to the GAA ground's car park where you can witness the above scene multiplied by one thousand.

It harks back to the days when we were all too poor even to think of eating in a café. So poor, in fact, were we that we couldn't afford to buy wrappers to keep the sambos fresh, so we used the one the bread came in. Of course, with the advent of the Celtic Tiger it was to be expected that the tea and sambos would be replaced with Caffe Macchiato and Avocado and Prawn Wraps consumed in 'La Bistronomy Alain' or the likes. Not a bit of it. To a large extent we still prefer 'The GAA Boot Bistro'. There's just something about the flavour the spare tyre gives to the ham.

Leaving Mass during Communion.

Once upon a time in Ireland it was regarded as a Mortal Sin to miss Mass on Sunday or on Holy Days of Obligation. The churches in old Catholic Ireland in those days were so packed they resembled the mosh pit at a rock concert. Unless

you arrived early you would only find standing room in the aisles and even then you would have to say your prayers with some guy's elbow stuck in your eye, or if you were male and lucky, pressed against the rear of a nice cailín you fancied.

Yet there is evidence that many of us weren't quite as devout as we seemed. See, we all knew that the Mass technically ended after communion. After that it was just really the priest saying his farewells and thanking God for his goodness etc.

So in the melee to receive communion and with the priest's attention distracted, a large percentage of the congregation loved to slip away ten minutes early, usually so they could get a seat in the local, and, like every other Sunday, religiously get pissed for the afternoon.

28 Being the best fans in the world.

We do like to think of ourselves as the best fans in the world, especially in terms of our international soccer team. Whether the title is merited or not is moot, but the fact is that we do sing a lot at games, passionately cheer ourselves hoarse, turn stadia into seas of green and keep cheering our team right to the end, win or lose. Other teams' fans like to riot, burn down the stadium, hurl missiles at the pitch, cause matches to be abandoned etc. But Irish people

Gerrit Quast

basically couldn't be arsed with all that. It just sounds like too much hard work.

If only the team could win something every now and again.

 Giving directions to strangers, especially foreign visitors.

We Irish just can't help being helpful and this is no more evident than in our eagerness to point strangers in the right direction. And even if we haven't a clue where the poor eejit wants to go, we're likely to take a wild guess rather than appear unhelpful, the rationale being that even if you accidentally direct the visitor into a drug-infested, black-listed, no-go crime area where he or she will most likely be bludgeoned and robbed, the visitor will still have a soft spot for the nice Irish person who tried to help him.

Unfortunately even when we do know the destination sought, we have a tendency to reference multiple points along the way that are known only to other locals, e.g.:

'Excuse me sir, could you direct me to Murphy's Bar?'

'Sure, you see that Garda Station? Turn left there until you come to Mick's house, then go right past the post box and if you see a cow in a field, you've made a wrong turn. In which case you should retrace your steps to the river and if there's a man fishing there, ask him where's Murphy's and if he's not there, cross the bridge and turn right until you come to a green house at the top of the hill. You should be able to see Murphy's Bar from there, if there isn't a mist.'

Visitors would be lost without us.

Your Ma or Da greeting you with the phrase 'D'ye know who's dead?'

(See also 'Reading death notices in the newspaper or listening to death notices on the radio,' and 'Going to funerals.')

With most other nations the conversation starter usually revolves around the weather. And while that's also a popular opener in Ireland, equally common among the older generation is the priceless 'D'ye know who's dead?' So frequently is this question asked when you visit your parents

that you often wonder have all their friends, relatives and neighbours been exposed to bubonic plague or some virulent strain of yellow fever. They seem to have an endless supply of stiffs to employ as conversation starters. Anyway, you reply 'No, who?' and they'll say something like 'Mrs Kenny' and you'll say 'That's terrible, what happened?' and they'll say 'Don't know, it was very sudden.' The conversation will proceed like this for about ten minutes until you finally manage to steer the chat away from Mrs Kenny's tragic demise towards the more important question of what your Ma has cooked for lunch.

Using the phrase 'geddupdeyard'.

This phrase is most commonly associated with Dublin although its usage has spread to much of the expanded Dublin commuter belt (e.g. Cork, Galway, Sligo). For the benefit of non-Irish readers, it literally means 'Get up the yard,' and it is used to tell someone good-naturedly that you don't believe them, or as a refusal to some request they've made, e.g. *'Hey Fiona, flash yer boobs for the lads',* to which Fiona might reply 'Geddupdeyard!' Unless of course said Fiona wishes to display her bosoms proudly in public.

The phrase originated in the 1960s, supposedly

in the playground of St. Pius X National School in Templeogue, Dublin, where a child seen playing too near the busy road end of the schoolyard would hear a teacher yell out: *'Mick O'Brien! Get up the yard!'*

An alternative origin is that it was a phrase frequently spoken by the character Benjy in the 60's/70's TV rural soap opera, 'The Riordans'. As Benjy directed the cows into the farmyard with a stick it is said that he would frequently yell, *'Get up the yard.'* This led to the development of a common insult: *'Get up the yard, there's a smell of Benjy off ye!'*

And if you choose to disbelieve either of these explanations, the appropriate response is of course: 'Geddupdeyard!'

St. Pius X National School in Tempelogue, The very first 'Getuptheyard' yard.

Using the 'cúpla focal' to stress our Irishness.

The *'cúpla focal'*, again for the benefit of non-Irish readers, means 'a couple of words'. Little bit of history here. One of the tactics the English government historically employed to try to suppress Ireland was to ban the teaching of the Irish language, in other words they were trying to turn us into English people. To put that in perspective, to the Irish this was the equivalent of when the wicked witch in a fairytale turns a handsome prince into a toad.

So, revolted at the thought, we clung to many of our ways like a dog with a bone, but, sadly, over the centuries the Irish language inevitably went into decline. Yet because we're all still taught it (badly) in school, most of us can still employ a smattering of it and like to profess our Irishness by occasionally dropping the odd phrase into a sentence every now and again. A few examples of this would be:

'Sorry I'm late, couldn't get out of my leaba (bed).'

'The sex was great, go raibh maith agat (thanks).'

'There's no point me going out with you Mick, is mise leispiach (I'm a lesbian)

'That Noeleen one has a tóin an-mhaith (great arse).'

 Red Lemonade.

Unique to Ireland, it's pretty much the same as white lemonade except that it's a deep ruby colour, probably through the addition of a hideously unhealthy colouring agent. Still, we grew up with it and always looked down on clear foreign lemonade as inferior. It still causes the occasional mix-up abroad when Irish people ask for a 'vodka and red'

in a bar, only to be met with a blank, uncompre-
hending stare. Red lemonade also has one other
benefit. If you're a child and you don't want to go
to school, gargling with it turns your mouth and
tongue a deep, unhealthy scarlet colour, which is
gross enough to have fooled the odd Ma into be-
lieving that their little darling was unwell. Or to earn
you a kick in the backside as she sent you
packing to class.

Hot red lemonade was also commonly pre-
scribed as a remedy for a child's cold, so, naturally,
us 'cute hoor' Irish kids had a lot more than most!

Laughing at foreign journalists mispronouncing Irish stuff.

(See also 'Having names visitors (even English-speaking ones) can't pronounce.')

There was a TV series in the eighties called 'The Thorn Birds' that featured a sheep station in the Australian outback named after Drogheda in County Louth. The only problem was that although the characters had Irish roots, mysteriously, not one of them could pronounce Drogheda, so they went through the entire series calling the place Drog-eeda. Of course, we're as guilty of mispronouncing foreign names as anyone, but we do love to chuckle with a vaguely superior air at foreigners trying desperately to get their tongues around certain Irish names or words. Their pronunciation of other place names had us rolling in the aisles – Dun Laoghaire became Dun Lo-ig-hera, Youghal somehow rhymed with Dougal and Cobh became Cobb.

In the political sphere the most common

offences were pronouncing Charles Haughey as Charles Hockey, Proinsias de Rossa as Pro-ins-ee-as de Rosa and the Dáil as the Dale. Political parties fared little better, with Fianna Fáil having the second half of their name pronounced as the word meaning 'not to succeed', and Fine Gael came out sounding like a very good high wind.

And how we sniggered when a BBC commentator once called the Garda Síochána rowing team the Garda Sigh-o-kanna. Let's hope they never have reason to report from Muck-anaghederdauhaulia in County Galway.

Boasting about how late your local stays open after official closing time.

(See also 'Being locked into a pub,' and 'Ordering multiple pints at last orders').

The licensing hours for Ireland's public houses have become a bit more liberal in recent times, but it still remains a nationwide sport to brag about how your local lets you stay on the premises way past official closing time. You will hear stories of people still getting served drink two hours after the barman called 'last orders' or tales of the pub doors being locked and the revelry carrying on until it's time for your cornflakes. Fellas will tell you that the Gardaí often come in and sit at the bar for a few pints, giving their unofficial seal of approval to the practice.

Undoubtedly some of these reports are exaggerated, particularly as the patrons of the bar are by then so sozzled with booze they can't tell what year it is, never mind what time it is. But we Irish hold it as a mark of prestige and pride if we have a particularly accommodating publican running our local. And in that regard, rural Irish publicans fare best – they are the true champions of the illicit after-hours drinker, held in higher regard than the sainted patriots who died for our freedom.

Better still, it is a well-known fact that in certain small rural communities, especially those that don't have a Garda presence, the pubs close their doors around midnight and not only serve drink, but distribute ashtrays around the tables, allowing the patrons to smoke away to their lungs' content. Now if you can make that boast about your local, you'll leave your drinking companions green with envy.

Irish speakers using English terms for which there is no translation.

For most people, learning Irish in school was a nightmare, particularly as the method of teaching it, for reasons beyond human comprehension, starts with the premise that you can already speak it fluently. Not a word of English shall pass your lips or you shall be cast into the eternal flames of hell! Of course any eejit can see the problems inherent in this system, but the Masonic-type powers-that-be have decreed that we should persist with this nonsense, probably because they don't actually want anyone else to learn to speak fluently so they can maintain their air of superiority.

So while our general populace may not exactly have happy memories of learning our native language, we do all have great craic listening to the Gaeilgeoirs having to dirty their mouths with English terms for which there is no translation. Sometimes they've even tried to distort an English term or two by sort of spelling it phonetically and pretending it was Irish all along, e.g. guess what *'Tacsai'* means? (Hint: It's a means of transport) *'Rugbai?'* (Hint: It's a sport with an oval ball). *'Teileafóin?'* (Hint: It's a communications device).

But best of all is when the Gaeilgeoirí haven't yet come up with a translation so they're forced to use the English term as is, which is becoming a big problem for them in these high tech days. So if you're unfortunate to be within earshot of a rabid Gaeilgeoir, you're likely to hear stuff like this:

'Texted Sinead mé ar mo mobile mar go raibh mé ar an internet agus chonaic mé í ar Facebook agus d'fhéach sí cosúil leis an robot i Terminator 3. Péire boobs álainn!'

Felix 'O'

37 Collecting money after their First Holy Communion.

The happiest memory of Irish childhood. Most Irish people can still recall (even fifty years after the event) precisely how much they received from their various aunts and uncles and neighbours. In some cases this will be something like £3. 6s & 9d. For younger readers that would be worth about €4. (Let's just give the younger readers a moment to recover from their faint.)

Since those far-off days, the average amount now handed over is somewhere in the region of €1,000 and a couple of banks started special 'First Communion Accounts' – no, there is no depth to which they are not prepared to sink.

Whatever the amount, getting your communion money was the first real contact Irish kids had with a substantial amount of cash and so joyous was the experience, it almost made young Irish Catholics feel sorry for their Protestant compatriots. Naturally, the religious element to all this was completely forgotten in the desperate rush to accumulate wads of holy dosh. But the sums collected have by now become so obscenely large, rumours abound that the Minister for Finance is considering a 'Communion Tax', to help bail out Ireland's bankrupt economy. Only kidding.

Still, you never know…

Pretending they think U2 are crap.

Everybody in Ireland hates U2. It's hard to find a single soul who will openly admit to possessing a U2 CD or ever having downloaded a tune or attended a concert in Ireland (unless it was to see the support act). It's incredible to think that when U2 fill an Irish football stadium for consecutive days, all the attendees are overseas visitors.

And as for Bono? Jaysus, what a self-righteous, talentless, loud-mouthed gobshite.

In reality, the truth is the precise opposite of all

of the above. But Irish people just love to hate their most successful citizens (*see also* Begrudgery) and nowhere is this more evident than in the case of a band admired and loved from one end of the globe to the other. In some perverse way we believe that expressing our dislike for U2, particularly to foreigners, makes us *uber cool*. It's possibly a statement of our wish to put behind us the days when we had tickertape parades for Eurovision winners like Dana. Nowadays, when a band from these shores breaks all world records for sales or concert attendance, we love to shrug in a 'so what?', 'who gives a shite?' sort of way and then go on our way absentmindedly humming 'Stuck In A Moment.'

Being the worst road users in The Western World.

Ok, it's probably a stretch to say we love being the worst road users in The Western World, but we seem to take a perverse pride in being crap.

And we *are* crap.

A good example is the minimum safe distance to drive behind the vehicle in front. Now it's known widely that at 120 km/hr your car should be 100 metres behind. This will come as a big shock to most Irish drivers who up to now thought it was six inches. Another gap in our collective knowledge of safe driving practice is that Irish people, particularly rural Irish inhabitants, believe that the speed limit on narrow, twisty country lanes is reached when your foot cannot depress the accelerator any more. Urban dwellers seem to believe that traffic lights work as follows:

Red –   Stop.

Green –   Go.

Amber –   Accelerate to your engine's maximum tolerance levels.

Of course the *overtaking* lane on motorways is not known as the overtaking lane to Irish people, it's known as 'the lane that I can pull into, stay

there and drive at 50km below the speed limit while I sing along to my favourite CD and cause a snarl-up behind that stretches over the horizon.'

Before most Irish people do the driving test they genuinely believe that demonstrating their ability to navigate a roundabout single-handed while using a mobile phone with the other actually might earn them praise from the examiner.

And as for Irish cyclists. Traffic lights? What the hell's a traffic light? Having lights on your bike after dark? Now why would you need lights? And visitors beware: in your country you probably have 'cycle lanes.' In Ireland these are known as 'footpaths.'

The craic.

A mysterious phenomenon only found in Ireland, it is possibly the most sought after material in the country. The nearest parallel to 'craic' in terms of other cultures would probably be 'fun', but this word is only really distantly related to Irish craic.

Craic's origins are shrouded in mystery. Many believe it derives from the sixteenth century English word 'crack' which meant conversation, was used by the Ulster Scots and then adapted widely by the entire island, but with a much broader meaning. Others will tell you that it derives from the Irish word 'craicaire', which was a jester, joker or enthusiastic talker.

Whatever its origins, Irish people will go to great lengths in search of craic, which can best be described as a mixture of good conversation, slagging, joking, drinking, gossip, atmosphere, music, flirting, sex and various other indefinable

elements. Or it could be just one of these things. Craic isn't limited to the pub but can occur spontaneously in the workplace, the kitchen, the street or frequently in the bedroom.

Many phrases have been coined around the word 'craic', among the commonest being:

'How's the craic?' which is a greeting.

'Was it any craic?' meaning 'was it any good?'

'What's the craic?' meaning 'what's going on?'

'The craic was ninety,' meaning 'it was brilliant fun.'

'You're great craic!' meaning 'you're very enjoyable company.'

There is even a website to rival Facebook known as 'Craicbook', but one suspects Mark Zuckerberg won't be losing any sleep.

Depending on where you're from, slagging Jackeens or Culchies.

For the benefit of overseas readers, a 'Jackeen' is a person from Dublin and a 'Culchie' is someone from rural Ireland, and since time immemorial the two groups have been engaged in a war of words, or more accurately have been verbally abusing each other, usually, it has to be said, in a good-natured way.

The Culchies slag the Jackeens principally on the grounds that Dubliners really want to be English at heart – they are 'west-Brits'. One theory of the origin of 'Jackeen' seems to support this, in that it derives from the way Dubs waved Union Jacks when a British monarch visited, thus 'jackeen' meant 'little Brit'. Another possible origin is the nineteenth century word 'jackeen' which meant 'a self-assertive worthless man'. Country folk love to rib Dubs about their Union Jack-waving past, which is just about the most insulting thing you can say to any Irish man or woman. Jackeens are also portrayed as uncouth, hooligan, delinquent types as likely to stab you in the eye with a screw-driver as say hello.

Culchies, on the other hand, are, according to Dubs, a bunch of unsophisticated, muck-loving eejits who think Sherlock Holmes is the name of a housing estate. The word's origins are equally un-clear, possibly deriving from the word 'agriculture'. Another theory is that it comes from the Irish name for Kiltimagh in County Mayo, which is Coillte Mach, or simply from 'coillte' (the 'te' pronounced like 'ch'), which means forest. In other words culchies are a bunch of wild men and women who inhabit woodlands.

Whatever the origins of either, one of our favourite pastimes is to exchange abusive banter about our respective backgrounds. Culchies will

Culchie

Jackeen

delight in claiming that Dublin made a bid for the Olympics but were turned down because the Jackeens had proposed lighting the Olympic flame by throwing a petrol bomb. Dubs will respond by inquiring of their rural friend if his wife weighs more than his tractor. To which the rural person will relate the tale of the doctor asking the Jackeen where he was bleeding from, only to get the response 'From bleedin' Dublin.' At which point the Jackeen will describe a Culchie on a bike as a dope peddlar.

And so on and so forth ad infinitum…

Oddball sandwiches.

Having already touched on the Irish delicacy known as 'The Tayto Crisp Sandwich', it's worth exploring the other slightly wacky sandwiches to which we're partial.

Perhaps the oddest of these are the sugar sandwiches, which must be made with white sliced pan. They can be made simply by sprinkling a couple of dessert spoons of white sugar directly on to the bread, or if you're really keen on developing heart disease, the bread should be coated in a thick layer of butter first. Are usually made as a substitute for dessert or cake, when none available. What can you say, except 'sweet Jaysus'.

Banana sandwiches are also common. Very tasty when eaten fresh, but many Irish people will have childhood memories of opening their school lunchbox to find that the banana their mother put in their sambos that morning had turned brown and been squashed under the weight of a bottle of milk or something, leaving them with a repulsive, sagging, soggy lump of gunge to ingest.

Tomatoes are a popular sandwich ingredient the world over but only in Ireland are tomatoes often used as the sole ingredient. The belief among Irish parents seemed to be that these were best served while sitting on a beach, thereby putting the 'sand' in 'sandwich', literally. After the picnic, the kids would then dash back out into the sea, jump about for twenty minutes and then throw up the semi-digested tomato sandwiches into the surf. By the end of the day the water looked like twenty people had been the victims of a Great White shark attack.

Chip sandwiches are a particular favourite of one large section of the Irish population – those who frequently get completely pissed. For some reason, as we stag-ger home on a Friday or a Saturday night, many of us take the notion into our heads of popping into the local chipper and re-turning home with a bag of chips,  whereby we'll commence buttering slices of bread and heaping the chips into the middle, resulting in dripping, four-inch thick, artery-clogging sandwiches, which in our inebriated state we believe are somehow good for us, or will perhaps lessen the effects of the hangover the next day. Many of the consumed sandwiches are seen again the following morning.

Informality.

Next time you see a bunch of Irish men in penguin suits at some stuffy function on TV, on close observation you will notice their uncomfortable demeanour and the way their eyes shift left and right constantly. As they stand there, forcing large grins for the camera, you can only feel sympathy for them because you know that the one thing on their collective minds is getting out of there, finding the bar and having a pint.

The thing is, we Irish can only just about tolerate formality in very small doses. In other words, at heart we all want to be just one of the guys.

Our relatively classless society, referred to previously, is partly responsible for this attitude.

Formal dress and speech are regarded as something of an upper-class English institution, and as we find the British monarchy hilarious, well, we're not exactly going to go hell for leather trying to mimic them.

Formality, of course, is directly tied in to wealth, and in most other countries the wealthy spend their social hours in glitzy, ever-so-chic restaurants, wine bars and night clubs far removed from the great unwashed. The vast majority of Irish people would rather have their fingernails extracted with pliers than spend an evening in one of these establishments. Which is why many pubs and restaurants in Ireland contain an eclectic mixture of ordinary Joe Soaps and the most well-heeled in society and formality is collectively given a boot in the arse.

'Late Late Show' controversy.

The world's longest running chat show on RTÉ has kept the nation abuzz with talking points for literally generations. Whereas other well-known chat shows around the world rarely stray beyond the standard interviews with movie stars, writers, politicians etc, 'The Late Late Show' frequently explored alien territory in a way that would give, say, American TV executives coronary failure.

As a result the Late Late Show has been one of the key mouthpieces of social change in Ireland. Lesbian nuns in the 1970s, Gaybo demonstrating the use of a condom with his finger, interviews with mistresses of Bishops or Taoisigh, corrupt politicians, outraged archbishops, rosary bead-clutching protestors, loony militant activists breaking into the show live on set, trains full of contraceptives, you name it, the LLS has had it.

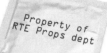

One of the early 'controversies' on the LLS, way back in the mid-sixties, concerned a Mr & Mrs-type quiz. When a Mrs Fox from Terenure in Dublin was asked by Gay Byrne what colour her nightdress was on her wedding night, Mrs Fox initially replied 'transparent' then on reflection informed Ireland that in fact she hadn't worn any night dress at all.

Cue condemnation from various apoplectic bishops that such 'filth' should be allowed on air. Telegrams were despatched from the Catholic

Church condemning the *'disgusting, disgraceful performance'* and Loughrea Town Council passed a motion describing it as a *'dirty programme that should be abolished.'* Thankfully it wasn't, and thanks to the likes of 'The Late Late Show', how far we've come.

Our colloquialisms.

While every country has developed its own local phraseology, the Irish revel in using the countless colloquialisms we've created down the centuries. In Ireland this is not only a means of casual communication, but another of the ways in which we express our national identity. We use these phrases so often it can sometimes appear to the outsider that although we're talking English, we're using some form of secret code that we are all given at an early age. Consider the following conversation:

'How's she cuttin'?'
'Oh howaya head, ah grand altogether.'
'So how's the head?'

'Banjaxed. I was rat arsed.'
'The state of yerwan last night. Did ye get yer hole?'
'Yeah no, made a right bags of it. Anyway she's an awful eejit, know what I mean like?'
'Yeah, poxy wagon. Anyway, my shout.'
'Fair play te ye. Let's go on the batter.'

Now if you're Irish this conversation makes absolute sense. Imagine for a moment you're from another English-speaking country and read it again. To put it simply, in terms of understanding it, non-Irish people wouldn't have a baldy, in fact the head-the-balls would be wojusly hockeyed.

46

Remedying every situation by putting the kettle on.

This topic could alternatively be titled simply 'Tea' as, Holy God, do we love our cuppa 'tae'. And no matter what calamity has befallen us, brewing up a pot of strong steaming tea will always remedy the situation.

Just lost your job? Don't worry, we'll put the kettle on and have a chat over a cup of tae. Your dog died? That's terrible, but you'll feel better after a cup of tae. A meteor just demolished your house? A  cup of tae will fix that. Husband just dropped dead from a heart attack? Cup of tae. Wife left you to join a cabal of lesbian Satanists? Cup of tae.

Whether in fact the effect is purely psychological or there really is any curative, mood-lightening effect in tea is debatable. As usual among scientists, opinion is divided. Some say it helps prevent cancer, others that it will bring on coronary disease, others that it slows your decline into senility etc. Take your pick. The caffeine content undoubtedly gives you a kick, which we probably mistake for a 'lift'. But one thing is certain, we've bought into its benefits big time. So much so that most surveys put Ireland as the largest per capita tea-drinking nation in the world.

We drink on average about four cups each a day of mostly Assam and Ceylon tea, which is black tea. And we like it strong. In Ireland we like our tea brewed until it's the same colour as our other national drink. Many of us are only happy with our tae when the spoon can stand upright on its own in the cup.

Climate change has apparently wreaked havoc in the tea industry in the last decade. Which is really worrying for Ireland. Forget about world oil reserves, should the tea supply fail, the place will grind to a halt.

47 Being loved by everyone on the planet.

Everyone wants to be loved and the Irish are no exception. Except we already believe that we are almost universally loved. But is there any evidence to support this assumption, or are we just fuelling our own sorry egos? Little or no studies exist to back up our belief, except those that rank us the friendliest lot on earth (*see* 'Waving hello to complete strangers on country roads'). But loved? It's probably better to start with who hates us and go from there.

Many would immediately assume that the English hate us, given our history. But anecdotal evidence suggests quite the reverse. Ask an Englishman which other race he hates and he's more likely to say the Germans or French. But us? Not a chance. The one group in Britain who are most likely to hate our guts are from a small part of Glasgow, and even among them the gut-haters are in a minority. For similar reasons, pockets of southern Irish loathing can be found in spots around Northern Ireland. After that you'd probably have to travel a long way to find another group who despise us. Our continental European neighbours think we're great craic, as do the Americans and Australians. Beyond that sphere, places like Kazakhstan or Uganda or Venezuela know as much about us as the Irish Department of Finance knows about finance, i.e. zilch, but they would probably have a sense of us as a poor little repressed nation and would therefore be sympathetic to us.

More generally, wherever we travel our first priority is usually to find a bar, talk for hours and get pissed. This has given us an almost worldwide reputation as a fun-loving bunch. And because, broadly speaking we can't be arsed or are simply too lazy to smash places up or start bar fights, we're also seen as a pretty peace-loving crowd. Which is great. Because the moral is, if we want to continue to be loved around the world, keep drinking.

Pictures of the Sacred Heart/Statues of the Virgin Mary.

In recent years Ireland has become not so much a Catholic country as a non-practicing Catholic country, an agnostic country, an atheistic country or a don't-know-and-don't-give-a-shite-country. But as recently as twenty years ago, almost without exception every Catholic home in Ireland was adorned with a large picture of the Sacred Heart and a statue of the Virgin Mary, which could vary in size from six inches to six feet. The homes of many of the older generation still feature these, but we've largely taken the view that these icons clash with the Scandinavian décor.

But many can still remember being met by Jesus's sad, appealing eyes as we arrived home every day and those same eyes judgmentally following us around the room, watching our every move. Even after your parents had gone to bed you could still feel those eyes boring into the back of your head like guilt-rays as you tuned into some naughty French movie late at night, or brought your boyfriend or girlfriend home for a snog and grope on the sofa. As the Sacred Heart pictures were traditionally underlit by a red light, it gave them an

eerie, spectral quality that would be enough to scare shite from a rocking horse, as the saying goes.

Having abandoned the living room, you would then be met by the face of the Virgin Mary, whose statue was usually positioned in the hall or at the top of the stairs. Cloaked in sky blue and white robes, head tilted to one side, hands open, palms forward, Mary seemed to be always asking 'My child, what sin have you committed now?'

Younger readers may scoff at such observations, but in various places around Ireland, the larger, life-size public versions of these statues have been observed by the faithful to weep, rock to and fro, bleed and even hover in mid-air. These popularly became known as 'Moving Statues'.

During the Celtic Tiger era the picture and statues were largely replaced with things like lava lamps. Which prompts the question: which generation was worse?

Claiming that Guinness always tastes better in Ireland.

Most Irish drinkers insist that when you get a pint of Guinness anywhere outside Ireland, it just doesn't taste the same. Is there any truth in this or is it merely a sort of pride thing – it's our national drink, so what the feck would some foreign bucko know about brewing it? And besides, we're the only true connoisseurs of the stuff. Well, according to the tour guide at the Guinness Storehouse in Dublin, it's an urban myth that Guinness is different elsewhere. Not that one doubts the guide's integrity or anything, but he's hardly likely to tell you that the stuff they export is crap.

Having said that, Guinness breweries outside Ireland undoubtedly follow the precise methods, use the same ingredients and apply the same care to making and distributing their product, so if there is a difference, where does it lie? Of course we're happy to accept all of that and still offer countless theories as to why it's different.

These include the following. The Irish water used in the home-brewed Guinness is softer, smoother, purer etc than anywhere else. The turnover here is so much greater, so there's a perception that our Guinness is 'fresher' and also that this requires the pipes in the pubs to be cleaned out more often. Then there's the pouring thing, which anyone who's ordered a pint in Britain will testify to – the barman does one pull and hands you a cloudy swirling frothy thing that finally settles down with a head that takes up half the glass – sacrilege.

There are as many theories as there are pints of Guinness drunk every day in the Dáil bar, which probably accounts for 5% of annual sales. In fact you will even find fanatical Guinness drinkers who claim that the quality deteriorates the further you get from St. James's Gate.

A more likely explanation for the widespread perception is that when you're having a pint in one of your favourite pubs in Ireland, you're so much more contented with the company, the atmosphere, the décor etc that you simply enjoy it more there. Sort of like playing on home turf, where we're always hard to beat.

President Obama claiming that the pint of plain is better here than anywhere else in the world.

Our daft road signage.

Ok, we may not love this aspect of travelling in Ireland, but it always provides us with some hearty laughter to brighten a long drive. Some of the signs are so poorly located and inaccurate you almost wonder if it's deliberate. But all over the country you will find incidents, even on main roads, of signs that say things like 'Cork 120km'. Fine. Then you drive 10km and meet a sign that says 'Cork 130km'. Now, unless you've just driven through some Stephen Hawking-type space-time distortion, any gobshite can see the flaw in the above.

You wonder how they could get it so wrong. Or is it just a case of –

'Hey Mick, I think we mixed up the last two signs, will we go back and replace them?'
'I'm not diggin' that bleedin' thing up again! We'll miss the match.'

Then there are the speed limit signs. These take farce to a new level. For years there was a sign on a six-lane section of the N7 between Dublin and Naas informing drivers that the speed limit was 60km/hr. This is the motoring equivalent of trying to stay upright in a slow-bicycle race. Conversely, all over the country you will find tiny back roads and laneways with speed limits of 60-100km/hr. Try taking the Gap Road from Lacken in Wicklow across the hills. This is more of a lane than a road and is only slightly wider than a car. In parts there is grass growing down the centre and in other

places the encroaching bushes claw at your car. The speed limit? *80km/hr.* You can imagine the conversation.

> *'Hey Seamus, we've no 30km signs left.'*
> *'What have we got?'*
> *'A few 100s and a couple of 80s.'*
> *'Ah sure feck it. Let's stick up an 80. Who gives a shite?'*

You have to laugh.

Slagging.

If you don't know what slagging is, you must be as thick as a heifer's arse. Now you know what slagging is, as you've just been slagged.

In loose terms, to slag means to insult, but usually in a nice sort of way. Irish people love to slag each other. We're masters at it. We'll say things like *'Sure you'd wring drink out of a floozie's knickers'* as easily as other nationalities will say *'Hi'*.

We love to trade insults like *'Jaysus, you're as sharp as a hurley,'* or *'Are you the sap in the family tree?'* Or occasionally we'll slag our pals in absentia with remarks such as *'Lucy's looks improve with distance.'*

But what is this obsession with giving others abuse? One likely theory is that our love of slagging is rooted in our inability to openly express affection for our friends and colleagues. Whereas, say, a French chap might greet a lady friend with something like, *'Antoinette ma chère, vous êtes plus belle que jamais,'* an Irish guy is more likely to say, *'Howaya Trisha, ye big wagon ye.'* Perversely, in this case the Irish guy's expression of affection is probably the more sincere, as the French generally do spout a load of pansy shite. (Only slagging).

Popular Irish slagging themes revolve around things like one's friends inability to hold their drink, how mean an individual is, how stupid they are or their lack of attractiveness for the opposite sex. So, although not all slagging is affectionate (see Begrudgery), mostly when we abuse each other verbally it's our way of saying we like each other. It's all a matter of tone of voice.

So to any foreign visitors who find themselves at the end of a seemingly barbed comment *(e.g. 'Ye big ugly foreign bollix')*, don't be too hasty to react negatively. If the person slagging you is smiling cheerfully and slapping you on the back, he really likes you. On the other hand, if he's swinging a chain and snarling, run.

Miming the National Anthem.

Surely no other nation on earth can mime their national anthem with as much pride and passion as us. It truly stirs the soul to stand at an international sporting event and observe fifty thousand Irish men and women either silently moving their lips in sync with the music or to hear them mouthing the nearest approximation they can remember of Amhrán na bhFiann that they learned in school. What's so stirring is that even though they haven't a clue what they aren't singing about, their faces are filled with emotion, contorted, infused with passion, as though they were each personally making a rousing speech to the insurgents on the morning of The Easter Rising.

The problem again comes back to our scant knowledge of the Irish language (see also 'Using the 'cúpla focal' to stress our Irishness'). Although we all learned Amhrán na bhFiann in school, or rather had it shoved down our throats by some fanatical Gaeilgeoir, it sort of went in one ear and out the other.

To help solve the problem, on the next page are two versions of Amhrán na bhFiann. The one on the left is the actual national anthem. The version on the right is the nonsensical gobbledegook that fifty thousand people are actually singing at sporting events.

The National Anthem...

Sinne Fianna Fáil

A tá fé gheall ag Éirinn

buion dár slua

Thar toinn do ráinig chugainn,

Fé mhóid bheith saor.

Sean tír ár sinsir feasta

Ní fhagfar fé'n tiorán ná fé'n trail

Anocht a théam sa bhearna bhaoil,

Le gean ar Ghaeil chun báis nó saoil

Le guna screach fé lámhach na bpiléar

Seo libh canaídh Amhrán na bhFiann.

and what people are actually singing.

Sheena Fianna Fall

Ataw phwee girl egg Eireann

Bween dar slew

Har tinn duh ronn egg coon

Fey unvowed veh sayer

Sean's tear air shin sheer faster

Knee augur vein cheer on naw vein trawl

A nuct a hames saw varna veil

Leh gan our Gael cun boss no sale

Leh gun na scrape fey lummock naw bill air

Sure live can egg Amhrán na bhFiann.

(Now cheer passionately)

Being locked into a pub.

(See also 'Boasting about how late your local stays open after official closing time'.)

One of Irish people's sinful pleasures, particularly in the past, was when official closing hours had arrived but the kind/greedy bar owner decided to shut up shop while the customers were still boozing away. This phenomenon has largely died away due to the more liberal opening hours of recent years, but still happens on occasion late at night, particularly in some rural backwaters. But in the not too distant past, pubs were obliged to shut their doors in the afternoons, Sunday being the most prolonged closure, and all over the country the locked doors and curtained windows of our public houses secretly concealed a sizeable pro-portion of the population happily guzzling away on their pints or vodka and oranges while the Gardai patrolled the streets outside, seemingly oblivious to the law-breaking boozers.

The thing was that once the doors were closed, you were stuck there whether you liked it or not – it

was entirely your responsibility to escape the
shut-in if you needed to be somewhere else. You
couldn't be let out again until official opening time
or you'd give the whole shebang away. Luckily,
most people were only too delighted to be trapped
within. It endowed them with a great sense of
mischief, allowing each
mouthful of Guinness to be, in
effect, like putting two fingers
up to the powers-that-be.
Somehow the drink tasted
even better then, as though it
was taken in the spirit of re-
bellion. You felt a strong bond
of comradeship with the

strangers around you, as though you were all
united in your defiance of the establishment and in
your pity for the poor unfortunates beyond the
walls who were thirsting for a drink.

And naturally 'being locked into the pub' usually
turned into 'getting locked in the pub.'

Winning one Olympic gold medal every twenty years.

It's a sad fact that, collectively, we Irish aren't among the greatest Olympians on the planet. The truth, if we're to be honest, is that as a nation of athletes, we're hopeless. This is not to disrespect the Trojan efforts of all those athletes down the years who have put in endless hours/day/months of training. But somehow we almost always seem to come up short. Perhaps it's just that as a nation, we're that bit lazier and we therefore don't produce the numbers of athletes required. And of course our governments have traditionally paid scant attention – and even less money – towards our athletes, usually only offering them support when they are successful against the odds and a good photo opportunity presents itself.

And yet, despite the relative emptiness of our Olympic trophy cabinet, our victories are all the sweeter because they're so infrequent. Most Americans, British, Germans etc could only name a handful of their gold medallists, so numerous are their successes. But here, because they're almost as rare as hen's teeth, most of us can rattle off the names of every one of our gold medallists like the days of the week. Well actually, they're fewer in number than the days of the week – we've had just five different Olympian gold-winners who share eight medals between them. But when it does happen every generation or so, Jaysus do we like to celebrate it. For a brief second we're the greatest nation on earth and the athlete is guaranteed eternal glory in our hall of Olympic fame, which sadly, is about the same length as the hall into the average three bedroom semi-detached house.

Our mammies.

The most powerful figure in Irish society is not the Taoiseach or the President or the head of the Central Bank. It is the Irish matriarch. Nowhere in the world does the mother figure have such an influential role as she does in Ireland, especially among the boys. Whatever Mammy says, goes, irrespective of whether you are six or forty-

six and have a wife and three kids of your own.

Most Irish brides quickly discover the reality that they haven't just married an Irishman, but his mother as well. The husband's mammy will sadly shake her head and frown at her daughter-in-law's attempts at cooking, decorating, finances and fashion sense and offer suggestions as to his particular likes e.g.

'Declan always likes to have the sheets tucked in at the bottom of the bed' or

'My Ronan always preferred warm milk on his cornflakes, dear.'

In fact our mammies' doting is largely responsible for the fact that many adult Irish males have no idea how to make a bed, boil an egg or change a toilet roll. We love our mammies because no matter how big a gobshite you are or no matter what terrible transgression you've committed, you know that Mammy will always be there to stick up for you and offer you comfort (unlike the feckin' wife, judgmental wagon).

'Mammy, I just got drunk and accidentally burnt down an orphanage.'
'Ah sure, never mind, son, these things happen. Sit down there and we'll have a nice cup of tea.'

But is the influence of the Irish Mammy on the wane among today's high-tech, high speed, much travelled, sexually liberated, modern Irish males? Quite the opposite. It seems Irishmen cling to their mammies' aprons no matter what upheavals society throws at us, as recent reports suggest that a third of Irishmen aged 25-34 still live with 'The Mammy', and the numbers are on the increase.

But what's the attraction? Is there some dark Oedipal complex at work in the mind of the Irish male? Or is it something simpler? Do Irish men merely like being spoiled rotten? Judge from yourself from the sample list below. During the average Irish male's lifetime the Irish Mammy will:

* Regularly enquire about your bowel movements.

* Lick the corner of a hanky to wipe away stains from your face.

* Always make a lovely roast on Sunday.

* Boast to her neighbours about your successes, even if you're in prison.

* Frequently ask if you're wearing clean under wear in case you have an accident and need to go to hospital.

* Bake the greatest scones in the world.

* Threaten you with an unmerciful hiding if you ever bring a Garda car to the front door.

* Say 'God forgive ye' when you say something she doesn't agree with.

* Frown at your girlfriends, particularly their scanty clothing and make-up.

* Always have your dinner, lunch and breakfast ready.

* Refuse to let you leave the house without a heavy jumper or coat, even in a mid-summer heatwave.

* Wash your dirty jocks without complaint and even iron them.

* Wear the expression of a martyr.

All of which explains the basis of the old Irish proverb that says:

'A man loves his sweetheart the most, his wife the best, but his mother the longest.'

Asking far-away relatives 'what time is it there?' or asking returning emigrants 'when are you going back?'

It doesn't matter how much time has passed since we last spoke to our relatives and friends in far-flung places like Australia or the Far East, or whether there is news of some great import to

impart, the first line of every long-distance telephone call from Ireland seems to be 'What time is it there?' Is it the case that, even in the age of the global village, we seem to have a fascination with the fact that while it's noon in Ireland it's pitch dark on the other side of the world? Or perhaps, given the fact that we can't open up with 'Terrible weather we've been having', 'What time is it there?' has become the long-distance conversation starter. It's a genuine mystery, especially as your distant friend or relation has already told you a thousand times that they're eight or ten hours ahead. Then there's our seeming inability to remember if you subtract the eight hours or add them on, which naturally has resulted in many an opening: *'Hi Mick, it's Fiona, what time is it there?'*, to which a disgruntled, drowsy voice replies: *'Four fuckin' thirty in the bleedin' mornin', ye stupid wagon.'*

On a related matter, we have a habit of getting up the noses of our emigrant friends and relatives as soon as they step off the plane by inquiring when they're going home again. The problem here, though, is just one of misinterpretation. Living far from home for any length of time, the Irish Diaspora lose touch to some degree with the Irish mindset. You see, whereas the returning emigrant interprets 'When are you going back?' as 'When are we going to see the back of you?', what the Irish person is actually thinking is: 'How many nights on the batter can we cram into your trip home?'

57 Taking pride in the fact that most U.S. Presidents (supposedly) have some Irish blood.

Barack Obama is the 44th President of the United States. Of that number, it is claimed that twenty-nine have some Irish in them. The fact that they also have some Italian, German, French, English, Scandinavian, Russian, Spanish, Scottish, Bolivian, Kenyan, Polish, Malaysian, Turkish and Faroe Islandese in them is of no consequence. What's important is that they can be somehow, however tenuously, tied to some remote backwater in the arse end of nowhere in Ireland and therefore look on the 'home country' fondly. Or, in other words, give us some money, support, tourists, jobs, visas etc etc.

Having a President with Irish roots also of course implies that in reality it is the Irish who are running the world and making all the big decisions. And while some scoff at the desperate searching for an Irish connection to the White House incumbent, many of us positively glow with pride when a link is established.

The latest of these of course is President Obama, who, lacking our virgin white skin tones and without a red hair in his head, at first glance doesn't inspire confidence that his ancestors once drove pigs through an Irish farmyard or sat singing rebel songs and drinking poteen in a hillside she-been. But where there's a will there's a way and sure enough a researcher dug deep enough to dis-cover that good oul' Barack O'Bama's great-great-great-grandfather was born in the village of Moneygall, Co. Offaly, which makes him officially 1/32 Irish, which as we saw, truly put the money in Moneygall.

And fair play to Barack O'Bama who downed an entire pint of Guinness with gusto, (unlike Her Majesty and Prince Philip, but then the poor Eng-lish never could hold their drink). Barack also even managed the cúpla focal, not as many as the Queen, but his were catchier. 'Is féidir linn' has ac-tually spawned a cottage industry of 'Is féidir linn' T-shirts, 'Is féidir linn' knickers, 'Is féidir linn' base-ball caps and of course there are the mugs. The

ones who buy this junk, that is. But Moneygall provided us with the proof that if anyone can
exploit a tenuous ancestral connection to a US
president, yes, we can.

Our most famous Irish-American President was,
of course, JFK, whose more recent descendants
had emigrated from Wexford. His visit here in 1963
was what really turned this Irish-American Presi-

John F Kennedy (Source: Wikipedia).

dent thing into an obsession.
Almost for the first time in the
modern era we were under
the world's gaze and what
craic we had, not to mention
the publicity the visit gave to
the tourist industry. And of
course U.S. Presidents themselves realised the benefits of
popping over to Ireland for a
quick pint on the way to a
world summit or something, as it did no harm at all
at all to their popularity among the millions of Irish-
American voters.

Since then we've had visits from a number of
Presidents keen to grasp the thin thread that links

them to the old sod. Richard Nixon, Ronald Reagan, George W. Bush and of course Bill Clinton, who claims an Irish connection through the Cassidy clan, justifying his dropping in to Cassidy's pub in Dublin's Camden Street. The fact that genealogists claim that no such connection exists is something we are happy to ignore. Besides, anyone who lands in Ireland and heads straight for a pub must surely have some Irish blood coursing through his veins.

Spice Burgers.

What the hell's a spice burger, we hear our overseas visitors crying. Well, for many years nobody actually knew. Or at least nobody who ate them knew. This was princi- pally because they were almost always purchased from the chipper on the way home from a night on the batter in the pub and really, who gives a damn what something is made of when they're rat- arsed? Then the unthinkable happened in June 2009 when the company that makes them announced they were to close. We were unified in our anguish at the loss of one of the modern nation's staple drunk food. *The Irish Times* summed up our distress with the headline *'Chippers nationwide mourn loss of spice burger.'*

Cue an outpouring of grief in blogs, chat rooms, the letters pages of our newspapers and on radio phone-in shows. It was only during this period of mourning that someone thought to ask what they were made of. It seems that many were 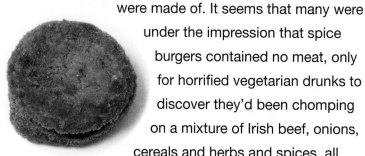 under the impression that spice burgers contained no meat, only for horrified vegetarian drunks to discover they'd been chomping on a mixture of Irish beef, onions, cereals and herbs and spices, all coated with a 'traditional' outer crumb.

Which is all a bit vague ... what herbs and spices exactly? How much and how lean is the beef? What's a 'traditional' crumb? As it turns out, the recipe's a secret, sort of like the Kentucky Fried Chicken coating or the third prophecy of Fatima. But more of that anon.

Such was the outcry from Ireland's drunken

Friday/Saturday night revellers that Walsh Family Foods managed to save the brand, the spice burger's Lazarus-like resurrection making headlines in Reuters and bizarrely, Dubai's *Gulf News*. Ireland's drunks could breathe a sigh of relief.

Since then the humble spice burger has hit the headlines again when it became the subject of legal proceedings, with Walsh Family Foods trying to prevent another member of the Walsh clan from producing his own version of the spice burger, claiming he'd nicked the 'secret recipe'. Eventually the dispute was settled amicably.

We allowed the banks to destroy our economy without a whimper. We allowed the politicians to burden us with debt for a generation through their incompetence with barely a raised voice. But threaten to take away our beloved spice burger? *Just try it, pal. Just try it…*

Dubs seeing Kerry being beaten in GAA. Everyone else seeing Dublin being beaten in GAA.

Nothing underlines the rural-urban divide in Ireland more than a GAA football match. If you're a non-Dub, it doesn't matter if your county has long since been eliminated from the All Ireland Championship, you can still passionately cheer for anyone but Dublin. Walk into any pub on a summer Sunday afternoon in, say, Donegal, and you will see lads and lasses in their county colours standing screaming at the telly in support of, say, Cork or Louth or Wexford – just as long as they're playing Dublin. Even passionate local rivalries are forgotten in the yearning for Dub blood.

If Cork are playing the Dubs, Kerry people will scream themselves hoarse in support of Cork as though Cork people are the most wonderful, saintly people on the planet and the Dubs are demons in Satan's army of evil. When it comes to GAA, it's essentially Dublin against the rest.

The reverse isn't quite true. Whereas 31 other counties hate Dublin's guts, the Dubs' ire is reserved for one – Kerry. This is probably because Kerry have beaten the crap out of Dublin in pretty much every game for the last thirty years. The golden days of the seventies when the Dubs had the upper hand over their great rivals are now a fading memory for the besieged million or so inhabitants of the capital, and new blue heroes are needed. But, as history has taught us, ultimately all Kingdoms come crashing to the ground ...

Dublin team psyching themselves up to face Kerry 26/8/07. (They went on to lose by 2 points) Photo reproduced by kind permission of Simon Fitzpatrick.

60 Telling friends you'll 'give them a shout'.

Non-Irish readers should not take the phrase literally. It doesn't mean that someone is going to suddenly emit a deafening yell in your direction and scare the shite out of you, as has been widely debated on international internet fo-

rums about Irish phraseology. 'I'll give you a shout' is in fact the Irish version of the wimpy French phrase 'Au revoir' and certainly in partings of friends has actually made 'Goodbye' virtually obsolete.

61 Committing the sin of illicit sex.

Please note that this section is not entitled simply 'sex', as of course Irish people love sex. Which nation on earth doesn't? What's unique about our take on sex is that up until rela- tively recently, most of us weren't allowed have any. For the benefit of more youthful readers, thanks to the Catholic Church, for generations sex was an eight letter word spelt M-A-R-R-I-A-G-E – and even then we were only supposed to indulge ourselves for the purpose of propagating God's children. Beyond that, sex in all its forms was banned.

The sex taboo was so extreme in the 1950s that the state used to employ a small army of people to snip lingerie ads from foreign women's magazines. The slightest, briefest peek of a bare boob in a movie led to howls of protest and censorship. Countless 'naughty' books were never seen by Irish eyes so officially we weren't even allowed to experience sex in our imaginations. Masturbation was a mortal sin, homosexuality an abomination and getting pregnant outside marriage was only slightly worse than being a Nazi

SS Obergruppenführer. Condoms were known as 'The Sheaths of Satan' and contraception in general was banned until the 1980s. Even the naked

beauties cavorting between the pages of magazines like *Playboy* could only be dreamed of by Irish males and smuggling one through customs was considered more risky (and shameful) than smuggling a case load of hash.

So when it first emerged that certain high profile members of the Church had been sticking their holy sceptres into the sheela-na-gigs, all bets were off. Irish men and women began to cast off the sexual shackles, not to mention their underwear, and indulge themselves in sinful hanky panky in their droves. For years we'd been staring up at the forbidden fruit and now it was like someone was shaking the tree. It was the sexual equivalent of the US repeal of prohibition – suddenly sex wasn't against the law.

And because we'd been so denied, for a while sex in Ireland was better than sex anywhere else on the planet. It was officially still a sin, of course, but if a bishop could get away with it and still get to heaven, by Jaysus the rest of us weren't to be denied.

62 Moaning about single mothers getting freebies from the state.

One of the most popular bugbears in Ireland, next to corrupt politicians and national bankruptcy, this topic commands more discussion time on the airwaves and in pubs etc than most others, (possibly with the exception of discussion on Miriam O'Callaghan's curvy bottom). The often warped thinking is that we're all toiling away, paying exorbitant taxes, getting pathetic services in return and what do we see? Some youngwan of sixteen strolling along the path pushing the pram-world's version of a Ferrari, dressed up to the nines, her pockets bulging with free cash she's just collected from the welfare office and then heading into her nice little rent-free house, all paid for from your pay packet. In popular imagina-tion she's also blissfully ignorant of where all her free stuff comes from. And allegedly she has no concept whatsoever of contributing anything back to the state in her lifetime – much like bank executives. The fact that a man had to have had a hand, not to mention other bodily parts, in the conception, and presumably is swanning about with ne'er a care in the world, looking for another sixteen year-old to impregnate, never seems to feature in these debates. Strange that!

 ## Fried Christmas Pudding for breakfast on Stephen's Day.

Another oddball Irish delicacy that would probably have foreigners gurning in disgust or at the very least scratching their heads. A big slice of Christmas pudding is fried in melted butter until the outside is caramelised and crispy, or some prefer it fried until it's actually burnt black. Gorgeous, and does wonders for the teeth.

On a slightly related topic, we also love calling 26 December 'St. Stephen's Day' as opposed to the British 'Boxing Day'. This is not because of some religious devotion to the martyr who was stoned to death in the Holy Land in 34AD (you knew that, didn't you?) but rather another way of expressing our Irishness, or rather our 'not-Britishness'.

64 The Angelus.

What? Love the Angelus? Are you bleedin' mad? We hate the Angelus! Why should we have to endure a loud gong-gong-gong twice a day, every day for the duration of our lives?

The Angelus, by the way, is a call to prayer, contemplation and to spread goodwill to all on earth, which explains all those weirdos in the television film that accompanies it staring blankly into space like they've been zapped by an alien hypnotic-ray gun. Let's just hope none of them are landing a jumbo or driving a JCB when the Angelus comes on and they're suddenly compelled to turn into zombies for sixty seconds.

Anyway, someone Irish must love the Angelus. And he or she must work for our national broadcaster, the only national television and radio network in the world to broadcast the Angelus. Although it is said that some remote Catholic

Jean-François Millet's "The Angelus" (1857 – 1859), Musée d'Orsay, Paris. (Source: Wikipedia).

radio stations in places like the Philippines also do the Angelus, as well as some crackpot, fanatical, right wing Catholic radio stations in the U.S., so whoever keeps the tradition going in RTÉ is in good company.

65 English celebrities who adopt Ireland as their home.

Our favourite English people are, of course, the famous ones who have decided to adopt Ireland as their home, or at least spend a large proportion of their time here. This provides us with irrefutable proof (at least we like to think it does) that Ireland is immeasurably superior to England. Among these obviously wise and discerning individuals are people like actor Jeremy Irons, director John Boorman, rockers Ronnie Wood of the Rolling Stones and Joe Elliot of Def Leppard and of course our favourite, Daniel Day Lewis, who has not only chosen to live here but has also officially become an Irish citizen, guaranteeing our total love and adoration of the man.

Of course the fact that lots of Irish celebrities have made England their home doesn't provide any counter-argument that England is a better place to live

than Ireland, as we can ascribe their actions to necessity and we all know that they'd all really prefer to be living back here in the 'auld sod than mingling with the 'auld enemy. So we'll continue to grant a céad míle fáilte to any other English celebrity who decides to come here. We're simply dying to demonstrate our wonderful hospitality. And besides, we could really use their money.

Ordering multiple pints each at last orders.

(See also 'Boasting about how late your local stays open after official closing time,' and 'Being locked into a pub.')

In most other countries when the barman calls 'last orders' a handful of customers will calmly walk to the bar and order one more drink for the road. In Ireland it seems we don't hear the words 'last orders'. Instead what we collectively hear the barman say is *'after tonight the sale of alcoholic beverages will be banned in Ireland forever.'* This terrible news naturally prompts a chaotic charge to the bar so that we can consume as much of our favourite tipple as our bodies will permit. The barmen are inundated with shouts of *'twelve pints of Guinness and six vodkas and whites please'* – and that's just for two people. In a blink the tables are overflowing with brimming pint glasses. In other countries 'drinking up time' usually means about twenty minutes. But because of the vast amount of alcohol that must be downed, 'drinking up time' in Ireland is usually long enough to allow a reading of *War and Peace*, not that anyone would be capable of reading at that stage.

Various commentators have proposed the

notion of extending pub hours to prevent the unseemly late charge to the bar. But we so love our late alcoholic gluttony that the mad rush would simply happen later, by which time we'd be even more drunk.

Sadly, this panicked, maniacal consumption of alcohol has several side-effects, like making you tell the same boring story over and over again or making you think you are whispering when you can actually be heard in the next street. It also leads you to believe that you are attractive to members of the opposite sex or to think that someone with a face like a bag of spanners is truly beautiful. Lastly, the multiple-guzzled-pint syndrome also seems to make many Irish people believe they have exceptional, Bruce Lee-like Kung Fu skills.

(Women) complaining about how crap Irish men are in bed.

Irish girls love to claim that Irish men are about as exciting in bed as a cold hot water bottle on a frosty February night. Allegedly, Irish men couldn't find a woman's important bits if they were given a map, directions and a flashlight. And even if they could, they wouldn't know what to do when they got there. Irish men aren't considerate of their partner's needs, aren't romantic and are about as sensual as a lump of turf. Irish men are also physically unattractive, all have beer bellies and sagging flesh and pay little attention to their physique or their appearance. All of which, perversely, is great news for Irish girls, as they just love to tell Irish men how brutal they are in bed as

it makes them feel all superior. Of course this suggests that most Irish women have some reference point by which they judge their

Irish boyfriends' performance, which logically means they've all slept with a variety of studs from every corner of the earth. And good luck to them in their research. The more international bonking the better.

But it must be asked, how much of this is a myth, invented purely to give Irish girls ammunition for slagging? Some scientific research is required to provide the answer. No sorry, we don't mean research that involves studying Irish couples in action and measuring the 'moan' quotient or anything, rather some statistical research.

In 2009, global research website OnePoll.com asked fifteen thousand women from twenty different countries to rate men of various nationalities between the sheets, (from memory that is, they didn't actually have to jump into bed with twenty different men and rate them). Anyway, the upshot, if you'll forgive the phrase, is that Germans were rated the world's worst lovers as they were too smelly, the English next worst because they were too lazy and the Swedes third worst because they were too quick.

Some of the descriptions given of the rest of the world's worst are worth a glance if only for amusement's sake: Americans were too rough, the Greeks too lovey-dovey, the Turks too sweaty (yeuck), the Russians too hairy and the Scots...wait for it...too loud! (OCH HEATHER LASSIE AH CANNY HELP I' AHM CUMMMMIN OCH AYE AYE AYEEEEEE!) Apologies to Scottish readers.

Joking aside, back to the serious scientific survey

stuff. World's best lovers? The Spanish. Then Brazilians, Italians, French and in fifth place … Irishmen! Ok, so the Irish guys are outside the medals, but at least all you Irish guys deserve a certificate of merit and probably extra marks for effort. Fifth in the world ain't bad, especially as all Irish men over thirty-five were denied the opportunity to get any practice for decades due to the fact that all our nice Catholic girls had their knickers welded on and fastened with a padlock.

So who knows, next time Irish guys could be on top, of the survey that is. Certainly Irish men are on the rise as lovers. They're the hard facts, girls. So save your moaning for the bedroom.

68 (Men) moaning about how ugly Irish girls are.

Until the dawn of the Celtic Tiger, Irish men were very content with their cailíns. Then suddenly these blonde, busty, perfectly shaped beauties started to appear everywhere – an invasion of eastern European babes that was welcomed with open arms by the men and with fire spitting from their eyes by the girls. Suddenly Irish men started to take fresh appraisals of their mots. Irish girls who previously had been rated 'a ride', were abruptly relegated to 'alright' status. If you were in the

'alright' bracket to begin with, you were now branded 'a minger', and unfortunate 'mingers' were downgraded to 'Medusa' status.

But was this fair? Were all these Polish and Slovakian and Lithuanian babes really so jaw-droppingly gorgeous? Of course not. Irish men just saw what they wanted to see and used their broad generalisation of the attractiveness of eastern European females as an excuse to slag their Irish wives, girlfriends and female colleagues, who are of course as beautiful or mingin' as their foreign counterparts. And besides which, Irish girls are much better craic. And of course Irish men ought to take a long look in the mirror every now and then. The vast majority of Irishmen are unlikely to see the next Brad Pitt staring back at them, more likely John Hurt in his famous 1980's role as 'The Elephant Man'.

Paddy's Day.

Despite what you may hear on the telly or read in the papers, we don't solely love St. Patrick's Day so we can spend it in the pub getting pissed. We love our national holiday because we love the notion that for one day of the year almost the whole world pays us some attention, and, generally speaking, toasts our prosperity. We adore the fact that performing troupes from France and Albuquerque and Greece and Azerbaijan and God-knows where else have come all the way to Ireland to march down O'Connell Street or the main street in Ballygobackwards wearing incredibly short skirts or gorilla costumes.

And how many other national leaders in the world get to have a private audience every year with the President of the United States in The White House? Answer: Zero. Cities and towns around the world dye their rivers and ponds and fountains green, guys with names like Abeeku

Onwuatuegwu wear giant plastic shamrocks on their head, and the prime ministers of far distant countries drink green beer and attempt a few bars of 'The Wild Colonial Boy.'

Photo: Gary Knight

God bless Paddy's Day. It makes the rest of the world green with envy.

Double-Barrelled Christian Names.

While Irish people generally tend to avoid the practice of adopting double-barrelled surnames, (principally because we think it would have us mistaken for British people, or because it all sounds too posh or a load of pretentious nonsense), we do love our double-barrelled first names, particularly in rural Ireland.

We are all familiar with hearing shouts of 'Howaya, John Joe!', 'How's she cuttin', Mary Anne?' or 'This is P.J. and his brother Tim Pat, and

his cousin Mickey Joe, and his sister Mary Jane, and their mother Anne Marie.'

Of course, double-barrelled surnames are rare, but not unheard of, and the nightmare scenario is when John Pat Kennedy-Lynch marries Biddy Anne O'Carroll-Shaughnessy. Even worse would be when Gaeilgeoirs Séamus Pádraig Ó Muircheartaigh-MacAmhalghaidh get hitched to Mairéad Seosaimhín Ó Raghallaigh-Ní Houlihan. But such a scenario is just too horrible to contemplate.

Asking favours in the negative.

You wouldn't do me a favour, would you?

Why do we almost always ask others for favours in the negative? Why don't we simply ask *'Would you do me a favour?'*

We all do it, unconsciously, every day.

'You wouldn't get me a cup of tea, would you?'
'You wouldn't lend us a fiver, would you?'
'You wouldn't fancy a snog round the back lane, would you?'

The thought of actually asking someone for a favour directly seems to frighten us. Or perhaps it's our cute way of subtly increasing our chances of success. It's as though we're first attempting to put a refusal into the other person's mouth by making a statement rather than asking a question, like: *'You wouldn't get me a pint while you're at the bar.'* By doing this we're implying that the person is a selfish bowsie, before we then offer him/her the opportunity to redeem himself/herself by tagging on *'Would you?'* In this way we're more likely to be granted our request.

So you wouldn't want to refuse an Irish person a favour, would you?

Herding cows or sheep with a hurley.

(See also 'Explaining hurling to foreigners'.)

A much-loved sport among Ireland's farming community is that of using a hurley to control their herds of cattle or sheep. We must assume that your average sheep or cow doesn't actually know what a hurley is, as distinct from, say, a stick or a golf club, other than to be aware that a belt from any of them hurts like the bejaysus. So we must therefore assume that driving a herd of cows along a country lane with a hurley stick is some sort of statement on behalf of the farmer, like the way

others will drive a sports car or wear a designer shirt.

What, precisely, are they saying to us? I'm an athletic type, a fine match for any country girl? Or perhaps they're hoping to be spotted by the local hurling coach who will be impressed by the way he can knock lumps off the herd. Or is it that the hurling team he plays for are brutal, and driving the herd through the gate is some sort of substitute for putting the sliotar between the posts?

It remains one of those closely guarded rural secrets, shrouded in the mists of county lore, and perhaps we'll never quite understand the mystery of the Irish farmer in the country lane with the sheep, the cows and the flailing hurley.

73

Deliberately going to the airport four hours before your flight so you can go on the lash.

Only in Ireland. Nowadays most people around the world hate airline travel. Security queues 200 metres long, passport queues just as bad, packed concourses, lost luggage, cramped seats, rotten food.

Luckily, in Ireland we still have the ancient tradition of soothing the pain of air travel by turning it into an excuse for a massive session, which is why Irish airport queues seem to sway from side to side. Unfortunately, on occasion, such craic is being had by all that we tend to forget the reason we're there.

And there's no funnier sight than six rat-arsed Irish lads and lasses staggering and stumbling desperately through the departure area shouting 'Where in Jaysus' name is Gate 36B?'

74 Telling foreigners that hurling is the fastest sport on earth.

Which is actually a lie, as in reality it's the Basque sport of Jai-Alai. It is however, the world's fastest field sport and we love boasting to visitors about the fact. Why? Well, we've bankrupted our own nation, destroyed our countryside with preposterous housing developments we can't sell, our politicians are generally corrupt and utterly useless, our society is riddled with cute hoors on the make, our principal religious orders were riddled with sex-fiends and our weather is totally crap and seems to be getting worse. One could go on. So what do we have left that we can boast about. Well … hurling is the fastest field sport in the world … so there … that's tellin' ye.

Going to funerals.

(See also 'Reading death notices in the newspaper or listening to death notices on the radio,' and 'Your Ma or Da greeting you with the phrase "D'ye know who's dead?")

More of a phenomenon associated with the older generation in Ireland, but attending funerals is still a popular pastime here, unless it's your own, naturally. Funerals are a great place to catch up with the more distant relations, see cousins and uncles and sisters-in-law that you never see from one end of the year to the other and find out what scandal they're up to.

After the poor unfortunate deceased has been consigned to the ground, the tradition of retiring to the nearby pub is a major social event where you first share anecdotes about what great craic etc 'oul Mick or Mary was, and then as the beer flows, the tributes slowly turn to venomous barbs about what a mean oul' shite etc old Mick or Mary was. Oodles of gossip are shared as the evening progresses and even the odd romance might blossom, oul' Mick or Mary already forgotten as newly met couples sneak out to the car park for a quick grope.

As social events, Irish funerals are in many ways similar to Irish weddings, the main difference being of course that there's one less drinker.

British royalty.

Ah, one can almost hear the screams of denial. British royals? We feckin' hate their guts! The living symbol of 800 years of British oppression! Should be all shot!

Yeah, yeah, right.

Two national TV stations broadcast the entire royal wedding live, and no less than 1.3 million Irish people tuned in. That's more than for the likes of the hurling final, Italia 90, the Rose of Tralee etc. And although the boys will insist that all of these viewers were women indulging in some 'wedding day fairytale fantasy', the number of comments being texted about Pippa Middleton being 'a right ride' tend to refute this.

And then there's the Queen's visit. Besides a handful of pissed hood-ies (who, incidentally, at one point struck up 'A Nation Once Again' but never got past the chorus as none of them knew the words), almost every single Irish man and woman wanted to personally embrace the old dear and show her what great gas we are and to show off our famous landmarks etc. The dismissive 'Ah sure at least it might be good for tourism' was often heard during the week, which was a way of appearing reluctantly to welcome Her Majesty while maintaining one's republican anti-royalist ethos.

In reality, all but the fanatical crackpots were delighted to see old Liz strolling around Dublin, Tipp, Kildare and Cork. And once she bowed her head in the Garden of Remembrance and followed up with the 'cúpla focal', that was it, we loved her to bits.

Pubs that also sell cornflakes, nails and peat briquettes.

'I think I'll drop down to Murphy's for a quick pint.'
'Could you pick up a loaf of bread and a tin of cat food while you're there?'

In the old days such a conversation wouldn't have been uncommon, as pubs, particularly rural ones, often doubled as the local grocery store, hardware, chemist, optician and bicycle repair shop. Or perhaps it was the other way around. Nowadays these are few and far between, but a handful do still exist and Irish people love to stumble upon them every now and then. Besides

finding them amusing, they prompt feelings of nostalgia in us, a yearning for days gone by, which if we paused to think about it were actually depressingly bleak. Still, there is something charming and uniquely Irish about ordering a pint of Guinness, a vodka and lime and a curtain rail.

Using the word 'after' when relating events.

If you're Irish, you're probably mystified by the above heading, because we do this so often and so casually none of us is even aware of it, yet it often leaves non-Irish people scratching their heads. Consider the following sentences:

> *'The government's after ripping us off.'*
> *'The banks are after bankrupting the country.'*
> *'Fiona's after having her arse re-shaped.'*

All phrases you might hear in modern Ireland on an average day. Take the last sentence. To someone from another English-speaking nation this sounds like Fiona is pursuing a course whereby she hopes to have her arse re-shaped, and not simply *'Fiona had her arse re-shaped.'*

Apparently, the reason we love this odd construction is to be found in the fact that the Irish language has no pluperfect (referring to an event that had continuing relevance to a past time), so when we began to switch our spoken language from Irish to English, we directly imported the construction used in Irish. We therefore add 'after' to the present continuous (a verb ending with '-ing'), so instead of saying *'We had gotten rat-arsed'* we say *'We're after getting rat-arsed.'*

So now you know what we're after doing when we stick 'after' into the middle of sentences.

Being unpunctual.

This just comes naturally to us. It's part of the Irish psyche, in the same vein as 'never do today what you can put off until tomorrow.' Our legendary lateness is a symptom of our famed laid-back approach to life. To us, punctuality is a game where you guess how late everyone else is going to be. So visitors, be warned: we love being late. And in Ireland punctuality is a virtue only if you like being lonely.

Putting stuff on the long finger.

For the benefit of anyone who doesn't know, the above expression means putting off doing something to an unspecified time, usually meaning never. It's an expression that is well suited to the Irish, because we just love putting things off.

It's possible the phrase has its roots in rings – if a girl had a ring on her middle finger she was neither married nor engaged and the date of her nuptials, if any, was some unknown hoped-for time in the future. But nowadays we use it for every conceivable situation, especially if we're required to do something unpleasant or energetic or something that's going to cost us money. What we're basically hoping is that if we put it 'on the long finger' long enough, it'll just go away.

A typical example is the fact that up until recently Irish learner drivers could simply renew their provisional licence indefinitely, with the result that half the country put the driving test on the long finger, and taking to our roads was like driving a bumper car in a fairground. Because we are generally such a laid-back lot, almost everything in life can be put on the long finger. Cutting the grass? Long finger. Getting married and having kids? Long finger. Put up shelf in the kitchen? Long finger.

But the most notable long fingerers in Ireland are undoubtedly our politicians, who have basically hijacked the long finger approach so they can get away with doing nothing. Evidence of various governments' dirty long fingers can be seen all around us in our deplorable planning, brutal public transport, criminal banking system and our pre-Paleolithic political institutions.

Most famous long fingerer of all had to be former Taoiseach Jack Lynch. During the 1970s' debate on the issue of contraception, which the incumbent government found decidedly uncomfortable, Jack Lynch famously admitted that they'd decided to put the issue of condoms on 'the long finger.' So it's possible that the roots of the phrase have nothing at all to do with engagement rings and the middle digit of your hand.

Farmers deliberately causing traffic jams by taking their time clearing the sheep or cows off a country road.

In Ireland this is the farmer's traditional way of showing those 'fellas from de big shmoke' just who's in charge in rural areas. Psychologists have analyzed the behaviour and believe it's all rooted in self-esteem and the need to be in control. Years of isolation in the countryside and working alone for hours in open fields have apparently resulted in farmers brooding interminably about their plight in life, while they imagine city slickers in the big cities having a rare ould time drinkin' and ridin' and shtuffin' their faces from dawn to dusk, and never doing a tap of work.

In order to balance the scales therefore, farmers regularly herd their animals out into country roads for no reason other than to cause monumental traffic jams. The poor sheep and cows are equally confused as they're driven first one way down a road and through a gate, only to be driven back the same way half an hour later all under the gaze of a strangely smug farmer, who every ten seconds, throws grinning, evil glances over his shoulder at the unfortunate drivers. 'That'll show dem, dem and der fancy cars and fancy clothes from Dunnes Stores.'

Psychologists also believe this behaviour should be permitted as it allows farmers to release 'mental steam', and should the practice of deliberately causing traffic jams with sheep be outlawed, the country's farmers would go insane en masse and the slaughter of urban-dwellers would be on a par with The St. Bartholomew's Day Massacre of French Huguenots in 1572. So next time a farmer keeps you stuck in a country lane for half an hour, just grin and bear it.

The Full Irish breakfast

This is the sort of thing that, should a nutritionist or dietician dream about it, they would wake up screaming in the middle of the night and require counselling for months afterwards.

Unquestionably Ireland's favourite meal, the Full Irish is distinct in many ways from the pale imitation that is the Full English. All the cooked ingredients of the Full Irish must be fried and

emerge dripping with grease from the pan and include sausage (2 to 4), back or streaky bacon (2), black pudding (2), white pudding (2), egg (2), tomato (quartered), potato cake (1), mushrooms (20), fried bread (2). In the past, fried liver was also included but this, like those who consume the Full Irish regularly, is rapidly dying out. Modern versions also include baked beans. The key difference with the Full English is that Irish sausages, bacon and pudding have a taste. Also, white pudding and potato cakes are exclusive to the Full Irish. Accompanying the above is heavily buttered Irish soda bread along with heavily buttered toast, and to wash it all down a big mug of Barry's, Lyons or Bewley's Irish Breakfast tea.

For those of us living busy, harried lives, in recent years we have developed the innovation of the Irish Breakfast Roll. To make this, take a large bread roll, slice it down the middle, butter heavily and cram all of the above in the middle (though not the soda bread or tea, which would make it very soggy). This can then be eaten while sitting in a traffic jam, or, to the annoyance of fellow passengers, on the bus or train. Cyclists have also been spotted eating the Irish Breakfast Roll as they weave in and out of traffic, as have juggernaut drivers on motorways.

Whether having the Full Irish on a plate or on the move, remember before you start to sprinkle it liberally with enough salt to exceed the annual safe recommended salt intake for ten people. Brown sauce or tomato ketchup is optional.

Scientists have yet to invent an instrument that

is capable of measuring the number of calories contained in this delight of Irish cuisine.

83 Driving miles to save 1 cent on petrol/ Driving to the North to save on the shopping.

We do love value for money. So much so that if word reaches our ears that the petrol station in, say, Carrick-on-Suir, is selling unleaded for a cent less than one's usual station, we're into our cars and off down the road quicker than you can say in-

ternal combustion engine. This seems sensible, until you realise that you live in say, Ballinrobe and the economics don't really hang together. But at least you get the satisfaction of denying the local rip-off garage your custom.

On a related matter, we also love to avail of the reputedly cheaper prices across the border in

Norn' Ireland. So off we go to buy our cornflakes, jacks rolls, frozen pizza, beer etc. We'll also purchase a few items of clothing while we're there 'to make it worth our while' and justify our boasting about our thrift and cleverness to our friends.

Having saved a total of about €50 on our purchases, we will naturally omit from our calculations the petrol costs (€20-€50), the toll charges (€10-€15) and the cost of feeding ourselves for the day (€50-€100) depending on whether kids were dragged along).

But there's the principle to consider. That'll show those greedy, overcharging southern Irish retailers! So there!

Having countless aunts and uncles.

In other countries an uncle is your mother or father's brother. An aunt is your mother or father's sister. In Ireland an uncle or aunt can include any of the following: mother or father's brother-in-law or sister-in-law, mother or father's brother-in-law or sister-in-law's brother or sister, mother or father's first, second or third cousin's sister or brother or father or mother, mother or father's close friends, mother or  father's drinking pals, guy or girl mother or father met on holliers five years ago, or any of the above's next door neighbour. In fact, in Ireland, every single other person in the country, with the exception of your mother, father, brother or sister, can safely be called 'your aunt and uncle'.

Must be an Irish 'family' thing.

Being drunk at midnight Mass on Christmas Eve

You have to wonder about us sometimes. What strange compulsions rooted deep in the Irish psyche possess some of us to do things like going to midnight Mass so rat-arsed that we can't recite our own name, never mind the feckin' Liturgy of the Word. The same scene is repeated in every village, town and city all over the land every Christmas Eve.

Practicing Catholic men and women are happily sitting getting sozzled in their local when someone realises that it's almost time for midnight Mass, and if they don't go now, they'll have to bleedin'

get up on Christmas morning with a hangover that would kill an elephant and sit through the interminable thing in agony. And if they don't go, of course, it's a sin. No consideration is given to the

fact that going to Mass barely able to stand, shouting about the local hurling team being crap during the Lord's Prayer or puking into the holy water font might actually be a sin as well … maybe even a bigger one. Not to worry about all that though, at least one can wake up on Christmas Day in agony but with a clear conscience. Well, holy God.

(Men) mispronouncing 'thirty-three' so that they can get off with English girls when on holliers.

The problem with Irish girls, traditionally speaking, is that they have always been seen as much more reluctant to jump into bed with a guy they only met about twenty minutes ago. English girls, on the other hand, at least in Irish men's eyes, seem to have long had the reputation as sex-crazy maniacs, particularly when on their holliers, who will have their bra and knickers off in Olympic record time. Naturally, armed with this assumption, Irish lads often target these loose hussies in the hope of some perpendicular refreshment.

And the favoured approach, it is said, is to get close enough to let them hear your accent, which, apparently, English girls find irresistible. Having engaged them in conversation, the Irish guy will deliberately use phrases like 'turty-tree', or 'I tink you're a deadly mot' or 'How's the craic?' (which even English girls consider forward until the translation is proffered). The belief is that such killer lines, delivered in our charming Irish brogue, will so excite the English girls that they will almost tear the lucky Irish guy's jocks off on the spot.

No slight is intended on the chastity of English girls by the above, who are undoubtedly temples of purity and sexual restraint. This is meant merely as a warning: the next time you're on your holliers and you hear an Irish guy saying 'turty-tree and a turd' very loudly, you'll know immediately he's not interested in your mind or a long term relationship.

87 Having names that visitors (even English-speaking ones) can't pronounce.

Many of the names that roll effortlessly off our Irish tongues seem to be spoken by foreigners as though they're talking through a mouthful of marbles or hard-boiled eggs. And how we love to tell them smugly the correct pronunciation and then laugh our heads off at their continued failure to grasp the subtle syllabification and nuances of inflection etc.

Let's look at a few simple examples of our Christian names. Take Donal. What could be simpler? Nope, wrong, non-Irish people cannot say Donal, they can only say the name with reference to Donald without the final 'd', or by stressing 'Don' rather than the 'do' which we pronounce 'dough'. Get it?

Another common tongue-twister for non-Irish folk is Grainne or Deirdre. They pronounce these as Grainn-ee or Deirdr-ee respectively. They simply cannot say the 'nyeh' or 'eh' bit at the end.

Tadgh? You now appear to be speaking in some obscure dialect of Swahili. Siomha? What is that? Dutch-Flemish?

Then we come to surnames. Even our anglicized ones are a mouthful, it seems. A lot of the trouble appears to revolve around the pronunciation of 'agh' or 'ogh' Thus Gallagher becomes Gall-ag-her, O'Donoghue becomes O'Don-og-hu-ee, Coghlan becomes Cog-huh-lan and so on. Other simple snigger-inducing pronunciations include Shea rendered as Shee-a and O'Shaughnessy which emerges as O-Sha-ugh-nessie. When they ask how to pronounce Ahern, we usually tell them to just say 'gobshite who destroyed our country' and everybody will know the name instantly.

But where foreigners (not to mention a few Irish people) really come unstuck is when we start intro-ducing them to the likes of Pádraig Ó Súilleabháin, Aoibheann Ó Ceallacháin or Mícheál Ó Muircheartaigh. Oh, how we chuckle.

Gaeltacht road signs confusing tourists

Our Irish-speaking community in the west of Ireland love to mount the occasional crusade against Anglicization of the Gaeltacht, one of the most obvious symptoms of which are the road signs. Fair enough, you say, but it also has the added benefit of giving us all a great laugh as we observe tourists wandering our by-ways in utter confusion as to where they're going, and the apparently strange rules of the road that exist in this part of the planet.

Imagine Herr Hansdieter Baumgaertner and his wife, Gretchen, from Witzenhausen in Germany, on their holliers in Galway, driving happily along on their way to Carraroe. Naturally, when they see the sign for 'An Cheathru Rua' they'll ignore it. Two hours later, bewildered, they consult their map and decide instead to pay a trip to Lettermullen but can only find directions to Leitir Meallain. They have the same trouble finding Ballyconneely (Baile Conaola) not to mention Clifden (An Clochán). Several frustrating hours later, Hansdieter and Gretchen, who had started out all lovey-dovey, are now yelling things at each other like *'Fick dich!'* and *'Verpiss dich!'* Not only can they not find their destination, but they've almost been killed ten times, having encountered informational signage telling them *Go Mall* (Drive Slowly) which they thought was a trendy shopping centre until they skidded off a sharp bend and demolished a haystack. Hansdieter didn't quite grasp the meaning of *Bothar Dúnta* (Road Closed) until he had to slam on the brakes to avoid driving off a cliff, and Gretchen was still pondering what *Oscoilt Cheilte* (Concealed Entrance) meant when the bulldozer emerged from the gate hidden by the trees.

Luckily, they survived their misinterpretations of Géill Slí, Stad, Críoch etc and returned home to Witsenhausen. And they did at least learn a little bit of Irish thanks to the Gaeltacht road signage – *Aire Leanaí,* they now tell their German friends, clearly means 'Beware of Falling Cars.'

Miscellaneous stuff
Irish people love.

Contributions to this book have come from Irish people far and wide, both at home and scattered to the four winds. The preceding entries were those that cropped up repeatedly, but lots of other stuff we apparently love but was not mentioned previously will ring a bell with many of us. These include the following, sometimes strange, sometimes quirky and sometimes downright bizarre 'loves':

* Referring disparagingly to some girl with the phrase 'the state of yerwan'.

* Knowing the tune to 'Wanderly Wagon' or all the words to 'The Safe Cross Code' TV ad.

* Pretending there is an art in playing the bodhran.

* Saying 'God forgive ye' to someone who has said something offensive.

* The bride and groom enjoying their wedding piss-up until 5am so much that they can't be arsed with the 'wedding night'.

* Deliberately wearing your county colours into your greatest rival's county.

. Telling someone that you could have got something they've bought much cheaper.

* Pretending you know someone in the IRA.
* Giving surnames to our pets, e.g Brandy Murphy, Rufus Byrne or Thumper McDonagh.
* Going for a few pints after Mass.
* The phrase 'Ah sure look it' being the solution to all bad news, no matter how disastrous.
* 99 ice cream cones.
* Telling your Ma you're going to Mass, then dossing for an hour before checking what priest said it, so you could pretend you went.
* Country fellas spitting in their hands before doing anything manual.
* Rubbing our hands together before eating a big meal of meat and two veg.
* Expressing our modesty when complimented with the phrase 'Ah would you go 'way out of that!'
* Using the bedside statue of the Virgin Mary as a jewellery stand.

We're an odd lot, us Irish, but you just gotta love us.

Tick the boxes to pass the 'Paddy' test.

☐ 1: Have you ever had Marietta biscuits with the butter squeezed through the holes?

☐ 2: Have you scraped shite off your boots with a stick?

☐ 3: Can you give the nicknames of at least 3 of our public statues?

☐ 4: Have you ever had a big lump of vanilla ice cream dropped into a glass of fizzy drink?

☐ 5: Do you insert swearwords into the middle of other words?

☐ 6: Do you say 'that's a grand healthy smell' when you get a whiff of cowshite?

☐ 7: Do you have a friend called Deco, Anto or Aido?

☐ 8: Do you read the death notices in the newspaper or listen to death notices on the radio?

☐ 9: You sleep in separate rooms when visiting your parents though you've been living together for ages?

☐ 10: Do you go to Dublin to do your Christmas shopping on 8th December?

☐ 11: You enjoy England being beaten (by anybody at anything.) Don't you?

☐ 12: Do you know some eejits with no teeth who have appeared on 'Winning Streak'?

☐ 13: Have you got a big family?

☐ 14: Do you love explaining hurling to foreigners?

☐ 15: Do you eat boiled eggs in a cup, mashed with butter?

☐ 16: Are you related to someone who fought in the GPO in the Rising?

☐ 17: Do you shout 'Yeeeeeooow' in the middle of traditional Irish tunes?

☐ 18: Do you change into your swimming togs under a towel on the beach?

☐ 19: Is Bacon and Cabbage your favourite meal?

☐ 20: Do you think 'begrudgery' is a national sport?

☐ 21: Don't you just love the 'grand stretch in the evenings'?

☐ 22: Do you boast that we were the first country in the world to ban smoking in pubs?

☐ 23: Do you wave to strangers on country roads?

☐ 24: Does nothing in the world compare to a Tayto crisp?

- ❑ 25: Do you say 'Ah no I won't' three times before you accept the offer of a drink?
- ❑ 26: Do you drink tea from a flask and eat sandwiches from the boot of a car while attending away GAA matches?
- ❑ 27: Was that you leaving Mass during Communion?
- ❑ 28: Are you one of the best football fans in the world?
- ❑ 29: Do you happily give directions to strangers?
- ❑ 30: Does your Ma or Da greet you with the phrase 'D'ye know who's dead?'
- ❑ 31: Do you say 'geddupdeyard'?
- ❑ 32: Do you use the 'cúpla focal' to stress your Irishness?
- ❑ 33: Have you ever had Red Lemonade?
- ❑ 34: Do you laugh at foreign journalists mispronouncing Irish stuff?
- ❑ 35: Your local stays open after official closing time.
- ❑ 36: When you speak Irish do you use English terms for which there is no translation ?
- ❑ 37: Did you get loads of dosh at your First Communion?
- ❑ 38: Do you think U2 are crap but have all their albums?
- ❑ 39: Are you're a crap driver?
- ❑ 40: Do you know how to have the craic?
- ❑ 41: Do you enjoy slagging Jackeens or Culchies?
- ❑ 42: Do you like chip sandwiches & banana sandwiches?
- ❑ 43: Do you tolerate formality in very small doses?
- ❑ 44: It wouldn't be Friday without the 'Late Late', would it?
- ❑ 45: Do you understand what 'Rat-Arsed' means?
- ❑ 46: Do you put the kettle on to remedy every situation?
- ❑ 47: Are you loved by everyone in the world?
- ❑ 48: Is there a Sacred Heart picture in your livingroom?
- ❑ 49: Guinness always tastes better in Ireland, doesn't it?
- ❑ 50: Don't you just love our daft road signs?
- ❑ 51: Are you partial to a bit of Slagging?
- ❑ 52: Do you mime the National Anthem at matches?
- ❑ 53: Have you ever been locked into a pub?
- ❑ 54: Are you proud that we win one Olympic gold medal every 20 years?
- ❑ 55: You love your mammy more than anything, don't you?
- ❑ 56: Have you ever asked returning emigrants 'when are you going back?'
- ❑ 57: Are you proud that most US Presidents (supposedly) have some Irish blood?
- ❑ 58: Spice Burgers are lovely, yeah?

❑ 59: Do you love seeing Dublin being beaten in GAA?

❑ 60: Do you give your mates 'a shout'?

❑ 61: Have you committed the sin of illicit sex?

❑ 62: Do you moan about single mothers getting freebies from the State?

❑ 63: Have you had fried Christmas Pudding for breakfast on Stephen's Day?

❑ 64: Do you stop what you're doing for the Angelus?

❑ 65: You know an English celebrity who has adopted Ireland as their home.

❑ 66: Have you ever ordered multiple pints at last orders?

❑ 67: Have you moaned about Irishmen being crap in bed?

❑ 68: Do you give out about about how ugly Irish girls are?

❑ 69: Does Paddy's Day makes you feel proud?

❑ 70: Do you have a double-barrelled Christian name?

❑ 71: You wouldn't ask favours in the negative, would you?

❑ 72: Have you ever herded cattle with a hurley?

❑ 73: Do you go to the airport four hours before your flight so you can go on the lash?

❑ 74: Do you think hurling is the fastest sport on earth?

❑ 75: Do you enjoy a good funeral?

❑ 76: Do you secretly like British royalty?

❑ 77: Have you ever been to a pub that also sells cornflakes, nails and peat briquettes?

❑ 78: Do you use the word 'after' when relating events?

❑ 79: Are you always late?

❑ 80: Do you put stuff on the long finger?

❑ 81: Do you deliberately cause traffic jams by taking your time clearing your sheep off a country road?

❑ 82: Do you wake up to the Full Irish Breakfast?

❑ 83: Do you drive miles to save 1 cent on petrol?

❑ 84: Do you have loads of aunts and uncles?

❑ 85: Have you ever been drunk at midnight Mass on Christmas Eve?

❑ 86: Have you ever mispronounced 'thirty-three' so that you can get off with an English girl when on holliers?

❑ 87: Have you got a name foreigners can't pronounce?

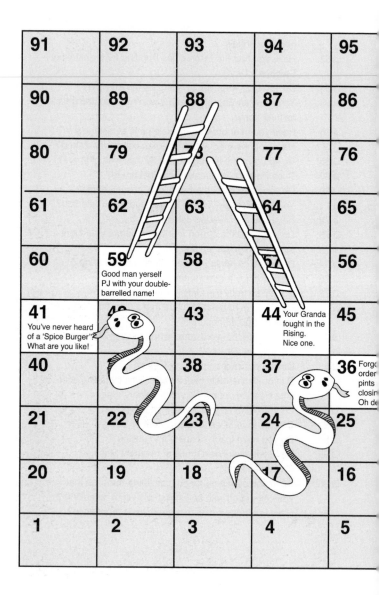

See how Irish you really are

91	92	93	94	95
90	89	88	87	86
80	79	78	77	76
61	62	63	64	65
60	59 Good man yerself PJ with your double-barrelled name!	58	57	56
41 You've never heard of a 'Spice Burger'? What are you like!	42	43	44 Your Granda fought in the Rising. Nice one.	45
40	38	37	36 Forgo order pints closin Oh de
21	22	23	24	25
20	19	18	17	16
1	2	3	4	5

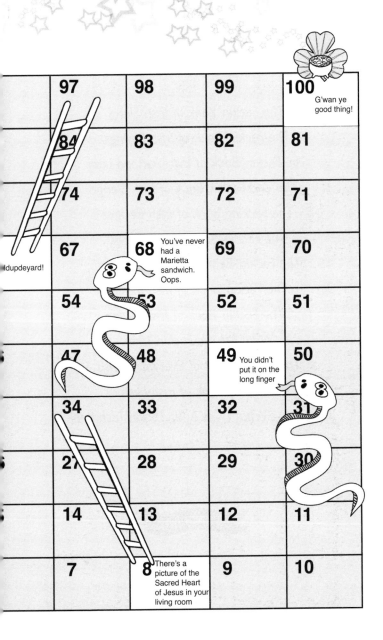

If you enjoyed this book, you'll love the *Feckin'* collection from Colin Murphy and Donal O'Dea:

The Feckin' Book of Irish Slang
The Feckin' Book of Irish Sayings
The Feckin' Book of Irish Sex and Love
The 2nd Feckin' Book of Irish Slang
The Fecking Book of Irish Recipes
The Feckin' Book of Irish Songs
The Feckin' Book of Irish Quotations
The Feckin' Book of Irish Insults
The Feckin' Book of Irish Trivia
What Are We Feckin' Like?
The Feckin' Book of Everything Irish
The Feckin' Book of Irish History
Now That's What I Call A Big Feckin' Irish Book